Collective Bargaining

Also by Walter E. Baer

Arbitration for the Practitioner (McFarland, 1988)
Labor Relations for the Practitioner (McFarland, 1989)

Collective Bargaining:
Custom and Practice

by
Walter E. Baer

McFarland & Company, Inc., Publishers
Jefferson, North Carolina, and London

British Cataloguing-in-Publication data available.

Library of Congress Cataloguing-in-Publication Data

Baer, Walter E.
  Collective bargaining : custom and practice / by
Walter E. Baer.
      p.   cm.
  Bibliography: p. 143.
  Includes index.
  ISBN 0-89950-402-7 (lib. bdg. : 50# alk. paper) ∞
  1. Collective bargaining—Case studies.   2. Collective labor
agreements.   I. Title.
  HD6971.5.B34   1989   88-34428
  331.89—dc19   CIP

Manufactured in the United States of America.

McFarland & Company, Inc., Publishers
  Box 611, Jefferson, North Carolina 28640

To my dearest Janet

Table of Contents

Introduction

The use of past practice to clarify what is ambiguous and to provide a given meaning to a collective bargaining agreement's generalities is a commonplace custom among arbitrators. Although it is customary for these professional decisionmakers to rely on past practice, the practitioner also can benefit largely from discussion and examination of the weight and effect given certain practices by arbiters. Arbitrators appraise the norms of conduct engaged in by the parties themselves to establish what their intent must have been under contract language that is susceptible to several interpretations, or is vague or unclear because of its broadly written character.

However, there is still another practice engaged in by some arbitrators, which rests on a more controversial foundation. What is referred to here is the proposition that the weight of past practice can be used to modify, alter, change or amend contract language which is seemingly clear, explicit and unambiguous. Much too often, from management's and sometimes also from the union's point of view, arbitrators deem it permissible, when confronted with a conflict between clear and unambiguous contract clauses and an established past practice, to consider that practice as sufficient to have produced an amendment to the contract. Although this is merely one of the problem areas which arises when one deals with past practice, it is probably the single one which has been the most annoying and disturbing to labor relations adversaries on both sides of the bargaining table. Providing clarity in this arena of organized confusion is certainly a formidable if not an impossible task, but an attempt will be made here to at least reveal the arbitral rationale which produced these divergent conclusions.

Also, an attempt will be made to delineate the factors and standards observed by arbitrators in determining whether in fact a fixed and established past practice exists between the parties.

In addition to the above-mentioned examination of "past practices versus clear contract language," another complicated and confusing area of past practice will be explored. Reference is intended here to the examination of cases where the labor agreement contained a "zipper clause" or an "exclusive agreement clause," and what effect, if any, their presence had on past practice claims. This is, regrettably, another aspect of the practice issue in which arbitrators find not only a difference in the criteria of decision, but in the results they reach. Perhaps there is no one enlightened path; nevertheless, our purpose will have been served if the critical examination of various arbitral opinions reveals some posts for guidance.

If nothing else, this book should emphasize the important role of past practices in the interpretation and application of labor agreements. The frequency with which problems of this kind arise and the significance given to some practices by arbitrators demand that both parties carefully observe the development of practices which may impinge upon the administration of an agreement. Both parties — labor and management — should share an equal concern over this troublesome matter. Common misconception holds that an arbitral determination preserving a practice invariably favors the employee and the union. However, official practitioners in the labor relations arena are familiar with the fact that, depending upon the nature of the case and its circumstances, either party may be urging that past practice prevail. For this reason, we cover cases where there has been both management as well as union reliance on the practice in support of their contention.

As it moves toward a conclusion, this book will provide the interested student of labor relations with a yardstick for measuring the extent and degree that a given practice is fixed and established. For the benefit of the management practitioner faced with inefficient, restrictive or costly practices, certain recommendations are forwarded which may enable him to bring about their elimination. The complexity of the problem areas which revolve around any case involving a claim of past practice makes the outcome dependent upon many uncontrollable factors and precludes against any guarantee of success to the practitioner (even if religiously observed). The best it can hope to do is to provide some broader insights in arbitral opinion and produce a more keen awareness between the parties of the tightrope they walk when dealing with this issue. Coupled with the posts we identify for guidance, these insights may lead us toward the light of understanding at the end of this foggy contractual tunnel.

1. Exclusive Agreement Clauses

A collective bargaining agreement negotiated between an employer and a union represents the compromise reached by the parties during labor negotiations leading to its consummation. During the discussions which finally result in a contract sufficiently mutually acceptable for both parties to bind themselves to its provisions by signing, each has attempted to meet the needs and wishes of the party it represents. On the one hand, the employer has sought to satisfy the needs of its management and its stockholders, while the union, on the other hand, has tried to satisfy the needs and desires of its members and the international union. Presumably, it contains what represents the sole and complete embodiment of the commitments each has made to the other for the duration of its term. But this is not to say that it always does, nor even that it clearly and precisely expresses what both parties understand it to contain, even if it presumably embraces all issues relevant to their relationship.

Such can be the contract product for a variety of reasons. One is that even expert labor relations authorities who have participated in the bargaining of the document can unintentionally create errors of draftmanship. Another reason which sometimes contributes is that often the final wording agreed upon is the product of the contributions of several people. Still another reason may be that because the parties have been unable to reach an agreement on a given subject, they have finally accepted wording which is ambiguous and susceptible to more than one interpretation (and since the wording does not clearly agree with the adamant position of either party, it represents a face-saving for both and a loss of face to neither).

An additional factor in the relationship that may produce an imperfect labor instrument is that the typical industrial plant is a dynamic organization with changing conditions and operations rather than a static one. Thus, the parties may enter an agreement that fits the operation it serves, but due to changing conditions during the contract's term, they find themselves attempting to bend it to fit a new situation. Also, no contract, no matter how comprehensive, can explicitly and fully cover all situations. Inevitably, a management representative will be

1

faced with the situation which does not appear to be embraced by his contract. And finally, even when a contract phrase is clear-cut in its meaning, practices may be initiated or allowed to continue which run contrary to the intent of the contract. I intend to deal with the problems these and other such factors create for all parties.

Who benefits most from the creation or existence of a past practice, the company or the union? This is an age-old contest with the final score yet to be tabulated. Needless to say, there are arguable positions in support of either contention. Recognition must be given by even the diehard who advocates the position that the union solely benefits, that occasionally management benefits also. Although begrudgingly given, this admission must be made in view of the revealed truth of the arbitration decisions which will be reviewed in this book. Many of these expose the fact that management sometimes defends its action on the basis of some supporting practice and occasionally does so in the presence of ambiguous language or in the absence of any wording whatsoever. More often, however, practices are used by the union as a means to obtain more from management than it could achieve by collective bargaining. This is the case since the union typically views the labor agreement quite differently than does management.

Management considers the agreement as the final point in the concessions it intends to grant for the term of the agreement. To the union, the consummation of a labor agreement brings it only to a temporary resting place in its quest for more. During the term of the agreement, the union will regularly and consistently seek to obtain more than it achieved at the bargaining table through its use of the grievance and arbitration procedures. This is its role and it is an understandable one. One of the ways open to the union to achieve this objective is to search out and find where management has established some condition or benefit not generally or specifically provided by the contract. Using the grievance and arbitration provisions as the instrument by which it seeks the established performance of the contractually uncovered item, the union seeks to obtain a grievance settlement or arbitration award which cements the condition or benefit as a now contractually covered item.

Management attempts to avoid this happenstance in several ways. First, it commonly adopts and practices a *residual rights theory* of management. Second, during negotiations it seeks the insertion of language into the agreement which limits the relationship of the parties to the expressed terms of the agreement and negates the influence of any unwritten understandings or practices which may exist. Third, it attempts to bargain into the contract a *zipper clause* which indicates by its phrasing that the union has had its opportunity during collective bargaining to present all issues and seek all concessions it has any interest in, and that failing to do so or failing to obtain what it had sought, it is now foreclosed for the term of the agreement from expecting to bargain with the company relative to any such covered or noncovered issue. This chapter will be primarily concerned with these two exclusive agreement provisions. But first, a few brief words regarding the residual rights concept.

In principle, what this concept consists of, as far as management is concerned, is that management has all rights it possessed prior to the coming of the union and prior to the existence of any labor agreement. Therefore, the provisions of the negotiated collective bargaining agreement containing limited restrictions on the company constitute the only extent to which management has relinquished its managerial authorities and discretions. In other words, only to the extent that the labor agreement limits, restricts or prohibits by some expressed provision management's prerogatives, is it so restricted. Therefore, it continues to possess all of the functions that management would be otherwise free to exercise if no union was on the premises. Generally speaking, the ritual of collective bargaining provides the union with an opportunity to convince the company to accept limitations upon the exercise of certain of its previously unrestricted managerial authorities. Where the union fails to attempt or fails to obtain such limitations on management's rights, the employer assumes it continues to possess all such rights undiminished. The residual rights theory holds that the employer retains the residue of all rights it has not bargained away. All rights not bargained away continue to reside in management.

This concept is often argued by managements before arbitrators on issues where the union claims support for its position based on some alleged practice. Where the union is seeking to obtain a benefit or condition, or its continuation, and it cannot discover supporting language to its case from the agreement, it typically resorts to a claim of past practice. Often such a claim is soundly based. Where the contract is entirely silent on the matter in dispute, it often brings to the forefront management's argument on residual rights. The company will often assume the position that it is incumbent upon the union to establish that a contract violation has occurred by requiring it to point to specific contract phrasing on the subject. Such contention by the employer is based on the premise that absent contractual provision which prohibits, restricts or limits management's right to take the action, whatever it was, management has preserved such right ungoverned.

The preponderance of arbitral opinion today holds to the following philosophical view on an employer's residual rights: "It is now a well established generalization that every employer continues to have all powers previously had or exercised by employers unless such powers have been curtailed or eliminated by statute or by contract with a union. . . ."[1]

While this is generally true and fairly typical of the concept endorsed by a majority of arbitrators, there are some exceptions. A silent contract, that is, one which does not provide coverage to a given subject, does not necessarily dictate that any uncovered subjects are automatically left to management's sole discretion. Therefore, it does not necessarily mean that any disputes which arise over matters not covered by pertinent contract language will be always resolved in the company's favor. Where this occurs, the customs and practices of the parties during the term of the agreement, and perhaps prevailing under prior agreements as well, may constitute a significant or even controlling factor in an arbitrator's final decision over the dispute.

Disputes between the parties may also arise over a subject dealt with in contractual language, but by wording or phrasing which is not expressed clearly and specifically. In other words, the contract may give coverage to the subject, but the particular language adopted by the parties may be vague, ambiguous and susceptible to more than one interpretation. Employers sometimes argue that they operate properly when they exercise managerial discretion to fill in such gaps which are caused by this defective draftmanship. Again, the residual rights concept is employed in this situation, positioned there by the argument that the ambiguity and vagueness of the language do not operate sufficiently to restrict, prohibit or limit managerial alternatives. Failure to realize that practices and customs under an agreement can become as compelling a part of the agreement as the written word has sometimes led to unilateral actions of management resulting in findings that were in violation of the governing contract. There is no question that the presence of a written agreement imposes certain limitations on an employer's previously unfettered prerogatives. It should be recognized equally as readily that the existence of certain practices and customs under that written instrument may also provide additional limitations on management's rights not expressly indicated by the contract's wording.

This is not to say that management is obliged to admit to the compelling nature of any practice so alleged by the union. Management should do so, however, if its own investigation reveals that the practice alleged by the union is a valid one, and has become a controlling factor in the handling of that subject matter. To aid the parties in their determination of the weight and effect to be accorded to any practice is the objective of this book. But from management's point of view, usually the wisest and safest course is to insist that the union find a base for its claim from some expressed provision of the agreement. Most companies, in the construction of the grievance procedure of their agreement, attempt to obtain a definition for a grievance which requires that for a claim to be a valid grievance, it must allege violation of a specific provision of the agreement as expressly written and provided therein. Their attempt to obtain such a grievance definition is in accord with management's viewpoint that the labor agreement represents the extent of their total commitment to the union. To further protect itself against additional encroachments by the union, the employer also often seeks a provision in the arbitration article which limits the arbitrator's authority to interpreting the contract as written and expressed, and prohibits him from adding to, subtracting from or altering the document in any manner when formulating his award. But, as we will discover, despite the presence of such grievance and arbitration terminology, and despite the vigorous argument of residual rights, practices and customs are often given compelling and controlling effect in arbitrators' opinions.

Before leaving this subject of employers' concern for management rights, it may be interesting to briefly examine how they declare such rights in their labor contracts. Management usually takes one of two approaches to protect its prerogatives during collective bargaining.

The first is to avoid any statement of such rights in a contract on the grounds mentioned earlier — that certain prerogatives are inherent in management and need not be fully stated and enumerated to exist and prevail. According to the advocates of this viewpoint, their concern is that a statement of such rights may be interpreted to not include other rights which are not fully enumerated, and thus actually operate to restrict.

The much more common approach is to include a management's rights clause in the contract which spells out as many prerogatives as can generally and specifically be listed in order to clearly establish the scope of management action which is to remain free despite the limiting obligations of the contract. This approach is often the subject of differences of opinion between those believing in a broad and general statement of managerial prerogatives and those believing in the detailed statement. These two subgroups are divided by the same considerations as divide the two major groups. What this means is that those supporting the general statement theory fear that a full and descriptive statement of rights may turn out to be restrictive (in the sense that rights *not* specifically asserted may be denied). The result is that a good many labor contracts try to solve this question by incorporating both a general and a detailed statement, or by adding to the end of a full and detailed statement of rights, a proviso which indicates that the list is *not intended* to enumerate all rights retained by management, and is therefore not all-inclusive.

About 14 percent of all agreements, mostly covering manufacturing industries, add such a proviso, commonly referred to as a savings clause, to the management's rights clause. A greater percentage, about 23 percent of all agreements, either add to or have in place of a management's rights clause, a statement to the effect that management retains all its usual prerogatives except over those matters for bargaining. These figures cited above come from a 1980 survey by the Bureau of National Affairs of 400 labor agreements covering manufacturing industries. In Table 1-1, the frequency with which the item appeared in a review of the 400 contracts is expressed as a percentage of the agreements.

General statement	77%
Direct working force	66%
Conduct business	65%
Control production	41%
Savings clause	
Specified rights not inclusive	18%
Rights retained unless	
contractually limited	23%
Rights detailed	
Company rules	18%
Plant facilities and location	24%
Determine employees' duties	17%
Technological change	17%

Table 1-1. Management rights provisions (manufacturing).

A review of trends and patterns relative to provisions contained in labor agreements shows an inclination over the past several years toward the insertion of savings clauses. The percentages above have moved up steadily, though not dramatically, over the past 25 years. Also, labor agreements negotiated by large, major manufacturers show that a substantially higher percentage of these favor the detailed statement of management's rights, plus the inclusion of the savings clause.

Past Practice Clauses

Management must realize that practices and customs are not established by the employees, nor are they established by the union. Such practices and customs first come into existence and then continue from one application of the practice to the next by the actions or inaction of management. This must be considered so since, under a labor agreement, management acts, the union reacts. The company is the party which has the right of administrative initiative. The union operates principally as a defense organization, with no right of administrative initiative under the labor agreement. Practices commonly develop when management makes decisions and takes actions (in other words, exercises its right of administrative initiative). If there is contract language which is clear and explicit, it perhaps permits only one position. But as discussed earlier, all contract language is not clear and specific and without vagueness.

Where the contract is clear, it probably allows those members of management who administer it only one direction to take in their decision making. But where the contract is silent or is susceptible to more than one interpretation (any one of which may be persuasively argued), management commonly fills in such gaps by exercising unilateral managerial discretion. Compounding this potential problem is the fact that the terms of the labor agreement are an umbrella over many, perhaps diverse, operations. Since widespread application of a common provision to different operations and departments brings many different circumstances, it is not uncommon for these management members to be not always singing out of the same hymnal. These are the circumstances which may produce different practices from one section of the plant to another, from one department of the plant to another, from one shift to another. Realizing this and the potential dangers it can represent to the company, many employers attempt to insert a past practice clause into the contract during bargaining.

One last point before turning to a discussion of such clauses. As already mentioned, management can be responsible for the creation of practices, often undesirable, by its inaction. This can result where management members responsible for administering the labor agreement acquiesce to conduct and behavior of employees and union representatives which are not in the best interests of the employer. This can occur irrespective of whether or not the particular practice allowed is given coverage by the contract, in whole, partially, or not at all.

For example, the employer's representatives may permit union representatives a greater degree of freedom and latitude in carrying out their union functions than is allowed by the contract.

Or, they may compensate or reimburse such union representatives for time spent during working hours on union activities related to the grievance and arbitration provisions where the agreement does not contemplate such payments, and perhaps fails to mention the subject whatsoever.

Management's agents administering the contract may permit employees to have idle but paid time during working hours for rest periods, lunch periods, wash up time, lining up at time clocks and other various activities. Such allowances may or may not be provided by the contract, or if provided, not to the extent acquiesced to by the company.

A listing of all the numerous and various problems such acquiescence can produce is almost endless. The point is that by management's *inaction* such can be the result. It must be termed as inaction since management possesses the power and authority to prevent it from happening in the first place, and has the authority to halt it once it has been allowed. The major problem resulting from management inaction which continues for too long is that once management decides to no longer be inactive, it may discover that it has waited too long to assert its authority during the term of the agreement.

One of the things the parties commonly do in an effort to give coverage to such practices is to insert a clause into the labor agreement which limits their relationship to the expressed terms of the contract. Representative of such a past practice clause is the following:

> This agreement supersedes all previous oral and written agreements between the company and the union. The parties herein agree that the relations between them shall be governed by the terms of this agreement only: no prior agreements, amendments, modifications, alterations, additions or changes, oral or written, shall be controlling or in any way affect the relations between the parties, or the wages and working conditions, unless and until such agreement shall be reduced to writing and duly executed by both parties subsequent to the date of this agreement.[2]

Such a provision is typically sought by the employer, hopefully, as a safeguard against the potential eventualities mentioned earlier. When the union submits a grievance which claims the continuation of a benefit or condition based on some alleged prior practice, management will often turn to such a past practice clause and cite it to support its denial of the grievance, and to seek shelter in its rejection of the impact of the alleged practice. This contention has enabled some companies to escape the encumbrance of an undesirable practice where they were fortunate enough to have selected an arbitrator who endorsed this theory. However, other employers have found that such defense was to no avail before other arbitrators. Often the difference between two opinions will be determined by the particular fact situation, the clarity or ambiguity of the pertinent contract language, the nature and extent and duration of the past practice, the bargaining history on the subject, and the ability of the contending party to establish that the practice in fact existed, was known to the other party, acted upon and acquiesced to. To make this point, a few examples are provided. A dispute involving the weight to be accorded a past practice arose under a contract which contained the following provision:

Article XXVII—Other Agreements
Section 2. The parties do hereby terminate all prior agreements

heretofore entered into between representatives of the company and the unions (including all past understandings, practices, and arbitration rulings) pertaining to rates of pay, hours of work, and conditions of employment other than those stipulated in this agreement between the parties.[3]

You can see the close parallel of this language to that cited earlier. The problem in this case concerned the company's assignment of boilermakers rather than carpenters to install and erect aluminum. The union contended that management breached the agreement when it failed to assign certain aluminum work to carpenters. To support its position, the union provided clear evidence to the arbitrator that custom and practice plainly established formal recognition on the part of the company of the jurisdictional rights of the carpenters to all such aluminum work. However, the company argued that any customs and practices which predated the current agreement were negated by the Section 2 language cited above. A careful review of Section 2 clearly indicated an intention on the part of the parties to terminate all past understandings, practices and arbitration rulings. Under these circumstances the question became, Would the reference concerning the elimination of past understandings in Section 2 eliminate those understandings which served to clarify ambiguous contract language, which continued to exist in subsequent agreements? The arbitrator said *obviously not*, because to eliminate understandings which clarify an unclear contractual condition would revert the parties to their original point of uncertainty which necessitated the understandings in the first place. He further concluded that understandings and practices which arise by virtue of ambiguous contract language remain in force and effect until such time as contract language which necessitated the understanding is changed. This he said was so, otherwise, uncertainty would result from a constant attempt to reach understandings over the same unclear contract provision, which would lead to insecurity regarding the sanctity of a promise. Therefore, he held that the terms of Section 2 did not terminate the prior understandings of the parties relative to the jurisdiction of the carpenters.[4]

Arbitrator Edgar A. Jones disposed of a dispute between the Fruehauf Trailer Company and the United Automobile Workers, where the contract contained both a past practice and a zipper clause.[5] The former provision (138) stated, "This agreement supersedes and cancels all previous agreements, both written and oral, and constitutes the entire agreement between the parties," while the latter (139) states, "No agreement, understanding, alteration, variation, waiver or modification of this agreement, terms, provisions, covenants, or conditions contained herein shall bind the parties hereto unless made and executed in writing by the parties."

The dispute involved a union claim that the employer had violated the job bidding provisions of the agreement and that a prevailing practice would be considered compelling. The employer sought refuge behind the above-cited contract provisions. In the substance of his opinion and award, the arbitrator theorized:

> The repeated execution of collective bargaining agreements which contain exclusive agreement provisions cancelling "all previous agreements" has no magical dissolving effect upon practices or customs which are continued in fact unabated and which span successive contract periods. Although not verbalized in the current agreement, such practices may nonetheless comprise a part of it as any of its written provisions....[6]

Thus ruling, he concluded that the company had violated the job bidding provisions of the agreement.

In fairness to arbitrators generally, it may be deemed advisable to make a few brief remarks relative to their decision making. Examinations of arbitral opinion invariably produce a finding of remarks by arbiters that the particular opinion was based "on the facts of the case." Divergent opinions from arbitrators on what appear to be very similar issues should actually be understandable to the practitioner. Differing viewpoints from one case to another result even where the labor agreement in two different and unrelated institutions may contain identical language. Despite these identical features, it is unwise to assume that arbitral examination of the language will yield identical interpretations. This is understandably true for a number of reasons, not the least of which is that the history of bargaining on the particular contract phrasing may have been quite different. Also, the contract's interpretation may have been applied in a different way by one employer and its union from that of another, different organization. Still another compelling factor may be the differences in practices and customs in which the parties have engaged. Consequently, an arbiter may, on a particular occasion, assert an absolute doctrine that the practices and customs of the parties, in the language they choose to adopt, actually represents the true agreement between them.

This same arbiter may turn around on another occasion and declare with no less conviction that his view of past practice is that it cannot alter the meaning of a clear contract provision. What is meant here is that many factors operate, perhaps in combination, to make each decision of an arbitrator relatively unique. It is not intended to imply that arbitrators are considered by the author to be innovators. These professional labor problem solvers recognize the compelling need for stability of labor relations between the parties. For this reason, an arbitrator, carefully researched by the parties before his selection and utilization of services, will usually exercise judgment in a very predictable way. The difficulty in examining arbitration cases dealing with past practice issues is that such cases invariably contain various of the aforementioned ingredients which can produce apparently different arbitral reasoning from one arbitrator to another, or from one case to another with the same arbitrator.

Now that this has been said, we will turn our attention to an examination of cases where arbitrators have given some weight and effect to a company argument based in part on a past practice clause.

A labor agreement between the National Can Corporation and the United Auto Workers contained a clause which read as follows:

> *Section 2. Inclusion of Subsequent Agreements.*
>   This agreement expresses all agreements and understandings between the parties. No subsequently negotiated agreements shall be of any force and effect unless in writing signed by the parties and made as memoranda of agreement supplementary to this agreement. Such memoranda shall terminate as of the expiration of this agreement.[7]

This employer had an agreement with a customer requiring it, under threat of financial penalty, to provide sufficient cans at all times to meet the customer's needs. Because of the directly connected and closely integrated operations of the two companies, the hours of production shifts were arranged to coincide. Following the customer's alteration of its processing schedule, it became necessary for this employer to change his working schedule accordingly. This resulted in an elimination of "wash up time" which the union protested as violating a long-established company policy, and company-union understanding.

The union alleged that the policy had been in effect for six years or more, and had continued under two labor agreements. It demanded overtime pay for the time that was involved and a return to the long-standing arrangement. Its contention was that the company could only accomplish such a change in a long-standing agreement at the bargaining table and not in the midst of a contract term. The agreement also contained a management's rights article and a clause divesting the arbitrator of any authority to alter, modify, add to or subtract from any of the terms or provisions of the agreement. Standing in his path of awarding to the union was Section 2, the past practice clause. This arbiter concluded that he would be exceeding his authority if he were to give any weight to verbal agreements or understandings reached in negotiations leading up to the agreement or subsequent to the execution of the agreement sought to be modified. He went on to say that if the parties had intended to give effect to any agreements or understandings reached in negotiations, they could easily have incorporated them in the agreement. In fact, they were obligated to do so if they intended that they should have any force and effect. If the arbitrator should, as the union urged, give consideration to "verbal agreements and understandings reached during negotiations as part of the contract," he would render meaningless said Section 2.

One arbitrator was faced with the requirement to decide the weight and effect to be accorded to two different practices which gave rise to two separate grievances under one contract. This single labor agreement embraced three plants of the employer, situated at three different physical locations. For a period of seven or eight years, the employer had voluntarily adopted the practice of giving an extra hour's pay for each day spent by employees on a certain type of work, even though no service actually was rendered for such pay. Upon the execution of a new labor agreement, the company discontinued this practice. The employer contended that the employees were not entitled to receive compensation over and beyond the regular hourly rate agreed upon by the parties in their new contract; that they were entitled only to pay for the actual hours worked; and further, that the additional compensation given to these employees discriminated against other employees performing the same tasks in the other plants operated by this same employer.

The union contended that such payment was now an established custom and practice in that plant and the employer had no right to change it, especially since there had been no discussion of such a change in the negotiations between the parties.

In view of the fact that such payment had never been made the subject of collective bargaining, and further that it discriminated against employees performing similar work in other plants that had never been granted such extra pay, and also because it was payment for services that were not in fact rendered and could not be justified, the arbitrator ruled that the company had the right to discontinue the practice.

The second question dealt with this same employer's practice of calling in an entire crew operating a large electrical shovel when it became necessary to make repairs on the shovel. Despite this practice of many years' standing, the employer began calling out fewer men on the premise that all were not required to perform the necessary work. The company contended that it had the sole right to determine how many men were needed on a particular job at a particular time. The company relied in large measure upon its management's rights article and Article 22, which stated: "All agreements heretofore made between the parties hereto are hereby cancelled and it is agreed that this instrument shall constitute the only agreement between the parties."[8]

At the arbitration hearing, the union testified that a prior oral agreement had been made between a responsible member of management and a union official to call out the entire crew when such work was necessary to be performed. The existence of this agreement was *not* denied or challenged by the employer.

On the basis of the management's rights article, as well as the inherent rights usually reserved to management, the arbitrator observed that the employer did usually have the right, regardless of past practice, to determine how many employees would be assigned to a repair job, unless in a particular instance, it had agreed to limit that right.

In relying on the above-cited Article 22, the employer contended that all prior agreements, written or oral, were abrogated. The union insisted that the employer did not have the right to change oral agreements previously made on this subject because the parties had never discussed or contemplated such a change. It contended that Article 22 merely cancelled all written agreements and written riders made between the parties and did not change the oral agreement pertaining to the point in issue.

On the basis of all the evidence, the arbitrator found that although management generally has the right to determine how many employees should be assigned to a particular job, it had limited that right by the agreement it made with the union which had remained in force for many years. Contracts can be changed by practice or custom where over a sufficient period of time the practice and custom amount to a mutual acceptance. In situations such as this, oral agreements may be just as good as written agreements and supplement the written agreements. One last point of significance to this arbitrator was that when Article 22 was being discussed during the negotiations, the union representatives inquired what effect the clause would have. In those discussions, it was clear that the employer did *not* mention that it included oral agreements. This, of course, did not prevent the employer from seeking a modification of such an agreement when the terms of a new collective bargaining agreement would be negotiated.

Another agreement, this one between the Breece Plywood, Inc., and the United Furniture Workers Union, contained the following provision.

Article XVI — Prior and Future Agreements.
   All prior agreements, either oral or written, are hereby cancelled, and this agreement shall constitute the only agreement between the parties. No supplemental or additional agreements between the parties shall be binding on either party, unless they have beeen reduced to writing and

signed by an authorized representative of the company and by an officer or officers of the local and international union.[9]

This same agreement contained a provision stating that, "There will be no change, during the life of this contract, in the past policy concerning the payment of a Christmas bonus." Under these clauses, it was finally ruled that the employer had the right to pay a bonus based on .5 percent of an employee's annual wages, instead of upon a 1 percent figure which had been used in computing the prior year bonus. Although the employer's past policy had been to pay a Christmas bonus, the amount of bonus and the standards used in computation had been varied at the employer's discretion from time to time. Moreover, it was significant that the employer had rejected a union contract proposal specifying the amount of bonus. This indicated to the arbitrator that the parties did not intend to bind the employer to a fixed percentage. The union alleged that the company had made an oral agreement with it to make another .5 percent payment at a later time.

Based on the language of Article XVI, cited above, the arbitrator would not consider this union contention. The union's failure to reduce the alleged agreement relating to the bonus to writing was fatal to the union's claim here. Under these circumstances, the arbiter did not have the authority to change Article XVI by holding that an oral agreement was binding.

The provision of the agreement presumably disposing of prior practices under another contract reads as follows: "No private agreement or understanding of any character or old established usage of any kind, shall have binding force unless contained in this agreement."[10]

The dispute between the parties here arose when the employer changed the method of pay for a certain group of employees from a piecework to an hourly basis, despite a long-standing practice of paying on the piecework basis exclusively. Relevant factors included the fact that the contract set forth both hourly rates and piecework rates for the affected employees' jobs; in the past, the employer had exercised its right to use either method of pay at other plants; and, other employers who were also parties to the same contract had paid the hourly rate to their employees for a long period of time. The union contended that management had waived its right to pay the hourly rate by its long practice of paying the piecework rate exclusively.

Two factors were essential considerations to the arbitrator's decision. *First,* the labor agreement allowed the company the latitude to use either method of compensation at its discretion. Both methods were specifically provided in the contract without any limitations as to the right of the employer to utilize either one. *Second,* the arbitrator was not persuaded by the argument that the company waived its right to pay on an hourly basis. The evidence as to waiver was conflicting and the best that could be said was that there was a misunderstanding as to whether or not the company relinquished its right to change from piecework to an hourly rated basis. The arbitrator remarked that he would be required to come to this conclusion even if there had been such an understanding between parties, in view of the clear and unequivocal language of the contract cited above.

Some collective bargaining agreements have provisions designed to ensure the continuation of particular established practices and customs. The labor agreement between Bethlehem Pacific Coast Steel Corporation and the Steelworkers Union contained a contract clause obligating the employer to continue an existing practice or custom not specifically mentioned in the contract, unless it could justify its elimination. The employer contended that the term "practice or custom" excluded those practices or customs which were "dictated by business considerations and operating necessities." The arbitrator rejected this argument on the premise that such a criterion could be used to exclude almost all, if not all, practices and customs and would virtually nullify the past practice continuation clause.

Whether the practice or custom fell within the scope of the clause had to be determined on a case-by-case basis. After arriving at these conclusions, the arbitrator went on to examine the merits of the dispute and ruled that the employer in this case was justified in discontinuing third shift assignments to certain jobs for a three-month period following production cutbacks on related operations. Such was the arbitrator's holding even though it had been a practice, previously, to maintain a third shift on these jobs regardless of cutbacks on other operations. The employer's evidence clearly showed that the work available for the jobs in question was reduced by at least one-third, or the equivalent of one shift, by cutbacks on other operations. Under this set of circumstances, the company was able to justify the elimination of certain prior existing practices.[11]

Where labor agreements have contained some type of provision assuring to some degree the continuation of past practices, arbitrators have used the following general principles.

First, practices under the agreement are sheltered and may not be changed or discontinued unilaterally by the company where the conditions surrounding the practice have not changed.

Second, where the circumstances and conditions surrounding the practice have changed, the practice often may be discontinued or altered in some form by the company.

Third, the practices under a labor agreement containing a clause guaranteeing continuation do not need to be the product of a direct authorization or management order.

Fourth, where management can demonstrate honest efforts to prevent the development of some practice, it may be ruled by an arbitrator that they have effectively prevented it from achieving the status of a bindng local working condition.

It is, therefore, safe to say that whether or not labor agreements, contain "silent" or "practice continuation" clauses, arbitrators have concluded that an established practice or custom is a condition of employment, which continuation is implied by the terms of a contract. Usually, they arrive at this opinion: (1) where there is convincing and compelling evidence that the claimed practice or custom was well known to the management and the employees, (2) it was seated in a mutual knowledge, (3) that it existed for a considerable period of time, and (4) that it continued unchallenged up to and beyond collective bargaining.

This result is not inconsistent with holdings by various courts that a contract includes not only the obligations expressly set forth therein, but in addition includes any implied obligations indispensable to effectuate the intentions of the parties.[12]

But one cannot apply the implied obligation theory blindly. In every case, the critical question must be whether the evidence warrants a finding of an inference that the parties tacitly agreed to the continuation of a specifically challenged practice.

Harry Shulman, one of the earliest outstanding spokesmen in the arbitration profession, in a case with Ford Motor Company and the UAW under which he presided as permanent umpire, stated:

> To imply an obligation is to find that both parties, not just one of them, in fact agreed upon it, even though they did not express their agreement in words, or that their conduct fairly leads to that result whether they thought of it or not. The propriety of the implication depends therefore on the circumstances of the case. Just as silence or certain other conduct may permit the implication, so also other conduct or expression may clearly negate it. If we assume that the execution of successive national agreements may imply, in general as well as by particular language, an obligation to continue local agreements or practices not mentioned in the national agreements, the question arises whether the claimed implication is proper in this case.[13]

Zipper Clauses

The provision popularly referred to by the parties as the "zipper clause" is locked in a great many labor agreements today. This clause is most often sought by the company rather than the union, although in some infrequent situations, the union has been as eager as management to obtain it. Management's interest in it comes out of the hope that such a provision will shut out the necessity for bargaining on issues uncovered by the expressed terms of the agreement. Its title is self-explanatory: It presumably zips the contract closed after the parties have consummated discussions leading to a finalized collective bargaining agreement. Saying that such a provision hopefully negates the obligation for bargaining during the contract's term is explained by the fact that the National Labor Relations Board accords it a varying amount of force and effect as a waiver specific enough to remove the obligation to bargain. Despite the presence of such a clause, Board decisions have turned on the particular fact situation, the individual and peculiar circumstances involved, the particular phrasing of the agreement, the practices and customs between the parties, the history of collective bargaining between the parties, and the company's good and bad faith.

The following clause is representative of a well-worded zipper clause provision, but, of course, there are numerous variations.

> The parties acknowledge that during the negotiations which resulted in this agreement each had the unlimited right and opportunity to make demands and proposals with respect to any subject or matter not removed by law from the area of collective bargaining, and the understandings and agreements arrived at by the parties after exercise of that right and opportunity are set forth and solely embodied in this agreement.
>
> Therefore the corporation and the union, for the life of this agreement, each voluntarily and unqualifiedly waives the right, and each agrees that the other shall not be obligated, to bargain collectively with respect to any subject matter referred to, or covered in this agreement, or with respect to any subject or matter not specifically referred to or covered in this agreement, even though such subjects or matters may not have been within the knowledge or contemplation of either or both of the parties at the time they negotiated or signed this agreement.[14]

Another clause of this type, which allows for bargaining on wages due to a wage reopener provision and results in bargaining during the contract's term, is stated below.

> This agreement expresses the complete understanding of the parties on the subject of working conditions, hours of labor and conditions of employment other than wages. This mutual understanding has been reached after many hours of collective bargaining and represents concessions which have been made by both parties in order to reach an understanding. It is, therefore, agreed that neither the union nor the company will present any demands or claims not included herein other

than as to wages during the life of this agreement, unless it is agreed by both parties that changes or amendments of this agreement are desirable.

The opposite of such clauses is achieved under labor agreements where the parties have inserted clauses similar to the following statement: "It is agreed and understood between the parties hereto that this agreement is limited to and embraces only such matters as are specifically set forth in this agreement and that all other matters shall be subject to further negotiations."

The latter two examples are provided only to show the various possible types of language adopted by parties in the absence of a true zipper clause.

When defending against some union claim based on past practice or a demand by the union for bargaining on some subject, supported by an alleged past practice during the term of the agreement, employers often join the zipper clause with the past practice clause and attempt to use the two of them as a shield against the union's claim. In some situations, the compelling force of customarily experienced practices may be diminished or eliminated *if* the contract language is sufficiently strong. And, where the past practice clause or zipper clause or both are clear and explicit, arbitrators have been known to dismiss the binding effect of a prior practice. For example, a particular written agreement provided the following statement.

> This contract represents complete collective bargaining and full agreement by the parties in respect to rates of pay, wages, hours of employment or other conditions of employment which shall prevail during the term hereof and any matters or subjects not herein covered have been satisfactorily adjusted, compromised or waived by the parties for the life of this agreement.[15]

Under the contract where this clause appeared, a bonus practice had been the result of negotiations between the parties and had been paid for several years. However, it had not been expressly written into the agreement and thus an arbitrator ruled that the employer could unilaterally discontinue it.

This, of course, is a representative example of a clearly and strongly worded zipper clause. It also represents the viewpoint of a particular arbitrator deciding a case in the light of its peculiar and individual facts. A different result would be derived under another collective bargaining agreement which contained a less strongly worded phrasing than "this contract expresses the entire agreement between the parties." Such wording was considered by this arbitrator to eliminate automatically only such practices as were in direct conflict with the contract's expressed terms. This arbiter said that practices were not necessarily matters for agreement.

Another clearly worded zipper clause appeared in the labor agreement between the Cone Mills Corporation and the Textile Workers Union. A dispute arose because the employer unilaterally instituted biweekly pay periods under its management's rights clause. The company had for many years compensated its employees on a weekly basis. Motivated by a desire to achieve economy in its payroll department and to improve the efficiency of its payroll system by evening out peak loads, it began to study a system of compensation on a biweekly basis in which employees would be paid on alternate weeks. During contract negotiations, the company advised the union that it was considering the adoption of such a system in the next year. The union made no objection, but suggested the desirability of first polling the employees to obtain their reaction to such a change. In May of the next year, the company posted a formal notice advising all employees that the weekly system of pay was being changed to a biweekly system effective in June. Shortly before the posting of this notice, the company advised the union of its plans, not for the purpose of obtaining the union's consent, but solely for its information. The grievance was thereafter filed, contending that the unilateral change violated the contract and a long-standing practice. The union cited its status under the recognition article as the sole bargaining agent in all matters pertaining to wages, hours, or other conditions of employment, and argued that the company had thus recognized that it must bargain with the union on anything referring to wages, hours, etc. The arbitrator noted that this contention ignored the following provisions of Section 12.

> The parties acknowledge that during the negotiations which resulted in the agreement, each had the unlimited right and opportunity to make demands and proposals with respect to any subject or matter not removed by law from the area of collective bargaining, and that the understandings and agreements arrived at by the parties after the exercise of that right and opportunity are set forth in this agreement. Therefore, the company and the union, for the life of this agreement, each voluntarily and unqualifiedly waives the right, and each agrees that the other shall not be obligated, to bargain collectively with respect to any subject or matter not specifically referred to or covered in this agreement ... except by mutual consent ... even though such subjects or matters may not have been within the knowledge or contemplation of either or both of the parties at the time that they negotiated or signed this agreement.[16]

In addition to being influenced by this contractual language, the arbiter also noted that (1) the contract was silent on the question of the frequency of pay periods; (2) the change in pay periods was not inconsistent with any right granted to the union by the contract; (3) that matters not included in the contract were not bargainable during the life of the contract; and (4) the unilateral action of the employer in paying on a weekly basis did not establish a binding past practice by the union's silent acquiescence to this employer-established policy. Under the above-cited clause, Section 12, the parties had agreed that they were not obligated to bargain for the life of their contract over any matters "not specifically referred to or covered" in the contract. Inasmuch as the frequency of pay was not specifically referred to or covered in the contract, the company was not obligated by Section 12 to bargain over the frequency of pay during the life of the contract. The agreement also contained another provision which stated, "Matters or subjects not specifically incorporated in the terms of this contract shall not be subject to arbitration...."

The stress in the contract upon matters not specifically referred to was also reflected in the above-cited provision. Joining these two clauses together, the arbitrator found reinforcement for his conclusion that the union's grievance was not arbitrable. A holding for the union in this grievance would have constituted the wholly unauthorized act on the part of the arbitrator of drafting the equivalent of a weekly pay provision into the contract. The failure of the parties to include any provision on the question when the contract precluded arbitration or collective bargaining concerning matters not specifically included, required that the arbitrator reject the union's position.

A contract between American Seating Company and the United Automobile, Aircraft and Agricultural Implement Workers Union contained the following clause:

> 59. This contract expresses the entire agreement between the parties hereto and it is mutually agreed that neither party during the term of this contract shall have the right to require the other to enter into negotiations or to entertain demands on any subject whether or not expressly referred to in this contract, except wages and insurance as expressly permitted in this contract and except alleged violations of the express provisions of this contract.[17]

This employer had implemented a scrap plan which had been in effect for about three years, whereby it made deductions from employees' incentive earnings for defective work, where the contract made no provision for such a plan. The union's theory was that since the plan was not mentioned in the agreement, it was automatically eliminated by paragraph 59 cited above. On this point, the arbiter opined as follows:

Collective bargaining agreements are not negotiated in a vacuum but in a setting of past practices and prior agreements. Such an agreement has the effect of eliminating prior practices which are in conflict with the terms of the agreement but, unless the agreement specifically provides otherwise, practices consistent with the agreement remain in effect. The written words of the contract may express the entire agreement as is provided here, but practices are not necessarily matters of agreement. Practices arise from custom, usage or continued toleration by one party, of action by another, which is not in violation of the contract.[18]

The arbiter then concluded that where a plan such as this one had been in operation for a considerable time, a party challenging it had the burden of proving that it did not conform to contractual requirements, or that its operation caused onerous results. Failing to establish either proposition, the union's grievance was denied. There is no gainsaying the fact that a certified union is the employees' exclusive representative to bargain for wages, hours and other conditions of employment. But once the union has negotiated for and agreed to certain such matters, its function of bargaining has been satisfied and completed, and it has no further power to bargain for the individual rights of individual employees on the matter of established wage rates.

It is true that there are agreements in which it is provided that the union will participate in the form of a joint review or otherwise in the administration of the contract; for example, in the administration of merit-rating plans. Where this occurs, the union has the right to bargain for individual wage positioning within wage rate ranges of individual workers. This was the nature of the holding by an arbitrator under a contract which provided for arbitration only of those matters falling within the terms of the contract. The grievance of employees who had been denied merit increases by the company was dismissed by the arbiter on the premise that operation of the merit increase plan was a matter not covered by contract. This particular contract contained a clause as stated below:

Only matters which fall within the terms of this agreement shall be subject to arbitration, and the decision of the arbitrator shall be within the scope and terms of the contract and shall not change any of its terms.

It also contained a provision stating:

Functions of Management. Subject only to such limitations as may be specifically imposed by this agreement, the entire management of the company and its operations is vested exclusively in the company.[19]

The substance of the arbitral opinion disposing of this issue was that the two above-cited contract clauses, operating jointly, precluded the arbitrator, in the presence of the silent contract, from sustaining the union's claim. Equally significant was company-presented evidence that the merit-rating plan had been established and in operation over a period of several years and had not been changed or affected in any way by the contract. In other words, the practice under the agreement favored the company, and the union was attempting to seek and obtain through arbitration what it failed to obtain during negotiations.[20] Before this arbitrator, this contract wording operated as effectively to foreclose the union from obtaining concessions over matters uncovered by the agreement as might a carefully worded zipper clause.

As stated before, the National Labor Relations Board views the continuing obligation of the employer to bargain differently than do the majority of arbitrators. It has recognized that the union can relinquish its right under the provisions of a bargaining agreement if it, as a part of the bargaining process, elects to do so. But for this to be accomplished, such a relinquishment must be in "clear and unmistakable" language.[21]

Silence in the bargaining agreement on such a particular issue does not meet this test. Courts have also held that they see no logical justifications in their view that in entering into a collective bargaining agreement for a new year, even though the contract was silent upon a controverted matter, the union should be held to have waived any rights secured under the Labor-Management Relations Act.[22]

The Board has ruled that an employer could not justify its refusal to furnish the union with information concerning individual wage rates on the ground that the union had bargained away the right to obtain the information. This occurred under a contract clause requiring the employer to disclose certain information, not including that in issue, and a further clause stating that the contract contained the entire agreement between the parties and that no matters would be considered which were covered by the written provisions of the contract. A three-member panel of the Board made the following remarks in this connection.

> The respondent's contention that the union bargained away the right to request the individual wage data is apparently based on the fact that the 1948 contract contained provisions requiring the disclosure by the respondent of certain information (not including that in issue here), and a further clause which stated "this agreement contains the entire agreement between the parties and no matters shall be considered which are covered by the written provisions stated herein." We need not decide, as the trial examiner did, whether this clause was operative during the period in 1950 covered by the complaint herein, for we are satisfied that,

in any event, the clause in question was not intended, and cannot be construed, as a waiver by the union of its right to obtain data necessary to the effective administration of a contract.

Thus, the Board concluded that this employer's refusal to furnish to the union a list of employees, identifying them by name, with their job classifications, hourly rates, and other wage information constituted a violation of Section 8(A) (5) and 8(A) (1) of the Act.[23]

Another sampling of National Labor Relations Board rationale is revealed in a case between the California Portland Cement Company and the United Cement, Lime and Gypsum Workers International union. The company contended that, because its 1950 agreement, as amended in 1951, contained provisions requiring disclosure by the company of certain information, not including that which was in issue here, the union expressly waived any right it might have had to this information. The pertinent portions of this contract read as follows:

> This labor agreement and the pension agreement together contain all the obligations of, and restrictions imposed upon, each of the parties during their respective terms.
>
> It is the intent of the parties by these two agreements to have settled all issues between them and all collective bargaining obligations for the term of the labor agreement (and for the term of the pension agreement relative to pensions), and that no change shall be made in either agreement prior to the expiration thereof except by mutual written consent and except as provided in Section 2 of Article 10 of the pension agreement.[24]

Despite the presence of this contractual provision, the Board held that it was dealing here with a right that derived from statute, without deciding that this statutory right may not be waived by a union. The Board did not, in any event, give effect to any purported waiver of such right unless it was expressed in clear and unequivocal language. Somehow they could find no such unequivocal waiver here.

As stated earlier, the bargaining representative's duty does not come to an abrupt end with the making of the agreement between the union and the employer, but collective bargaining is a continuous process involving both matters not covered by the existing agreement and the protection of the employees' rights already secured by contract.[25] The reason for briefly commenting on Board doctrine, as contrasted with arbitral opinion, is that the union may pursue this by filing refusal to bargain charges against the employer. In other words, the employer's contention that the past practice clause and zipper clause eliminate considerations of past practice and foreclose bargaining on uncovered subjects may provoke the union to this course of action. While it is possible that a party may concurrently pursue both the arbitration and unfair practice routes, I believe that it is inconsistent with the statutory policy favoring arbitration for the Board to resolve disputes which, while cast as unfair labor practices, essentially involve a dispute with respect to the interpretation or application of the collective bargaining agreement. The Board would be better advised, and the cause of industrial peace through collective bargaining would be better served, by deferring to the arbitral process and requiring the parties to resolve their differences by means of the machinery they themselves have designed and placed in their labor agreement.

I believe that the question of whether the parties, either by agreement, practice or bargaining history, have established their mutual rights and obligations with regard to a given subject, in the presence of an arbitration clause, should be a question that is answered in that forum and not before the Board. How much more specific a waiver could be expected to be achieved by parties in the collective bargaining process than the zipper clause herein detailed? If that phrasing does not meet the Board's test as providing an exclusive agreement, and an exclusive waiver of bargaining, then the question must be whether *any* language whatsoever would meet the test.

With regard to the question of past practice and the requirement to engage in collective bargaining relative to it, perhaps a few remarks of explanation are in order. Nothing contained herein is intended to imply that practices must continue indefinitely. As a matter of fact, later herein the subject of collective bargaining relative to the preservation or discontinuance of practices will be discussed. It is certainly recognized that practices or customs which create benefits, and these may take an infinite variety of forms, like other emoluments of value which accrue to employees out of their employment relationship, are a mandatory subject to bargaining which can be expanded or discontinued at the bargaining table. For this reason, employers are well advised not to unilaterally disturb that type of practice or custom.

Collective bargaining means sitting down across the table from the union and engaging in a give-and-take relationship. It means affording to the union in advance of the employer's discontinuance of the practice an opportunity to discuss the matter with the company and exchange proposals relative to it. The typical ritual at the bargaining table is for the union to start with a position of having nothing and seeking to obtain something. However, in most instances of collective bargaining relative to past practices, the union and the employees have something and the company wishes to bargain it away. If an employer can abrogate its obligations and responsibilities by unilaterally discontinuing bona fide practices from which employees derive a real benefit, and which have become established and accepted by the parties over a considerable period of time, then the collective bargaining relationship between these parties will be seriously strained. Many are the number of such items which often are not specifically detailed in the labor agreement. Of course, it must also be recognized that the give-and-take of good faith bargaining cannot occur after the employer has unilaterally acted to short circuit or discontinue an existing practice. The grievance action provoked by the company's unilateral behavior, and the discussions which then surround it, obviously cannot be considered as constituting good faith bargaining to which the union is entitled.

2. Clear Language Versus Conflicting Practices

You might assume that it is well-established that all past practices which are inconsistent with an express agreement between the parties must give way to the explicit terms of the agreement. This is, admittedly, the view expressed by a large number of arbitrators when dealing with a contract containing clear and explicit language on a given subject, with a long-established practice operating contradictorily to the contract's provisions. It is quite common to find among the many written arbitral opinions such a statement which calls this principle a well-established one. This author believes, however, the only thing that can be considered well-established in this connection is arbitral belief that the generalization is a well-established principle. Certainly, there are many doctrines and principles about the labor-management relationship which may be properly referred to as well-established in the thinking of arbitrators. But such cannot be stated with absolute certainty regarding contract provisions and the weight to be accorded a past practice which runs inconsistent with those expressed terms. It cannot be considered a well-established principle that clear contract language always prevails over a contradictory practice for so long as there are arbitration decisions rendered which are issued from unknown arbitrators or others who might be reasonably considered as inexperienced or neophytes to the arbitral process. If such were the case, their divergent and minority opinions might be written off as an immaterial expression from the uninformed. It is true that the decisions referred to here which run contrary to the supposedly well-established principle are not as numerously found in the written labor arbitration reporting services. Thus, in a strict comparison of the number of decisions in accord with the well-established principle, such different holdings would have to be construed as representing a minority viewpoint.

The significant factor that must be given substantial weight when examining the cases which produced different holdings is the character of the particular arbitrators whose opinions were expressed. It must be argued that this principle cannot be considered as well-established when

27

arbitrators of substantial stature, reputation and professional standing render decisions which recognize that in some cases a practice may be so compelling that it outweighs clear and specific contract language which provides for the opposite effect. The viewpoints of certain arbitrators who are considered by practitioners and their counterparts in the arbitration profession as ranking among the elite, should not, indeed cannot, be ignored, even though their voices may be fewer in number. Having said this, we will now turn to an examination of what, in terms of pure numbers, reflects the majority viewpoint on the issue of clear contract language versus a conflicting past practice. Before leaving the subject, equal time if not space will be afforded to the few whose voices must be considered as disproportionately loud.

Under a contract providing paid vacations for all employees having a year's service prior to a specified date, an employee who had the requisite service was considered by an arbitrator to be entitled to a vacation, even though he was on layoff on the date specified. The employer contended that employees had to be actively employed on the date specified to be eligible for vacation, and further, that no employees in the past had asserted a right to vacation if they were on layoff on the specified date. The company contended that on the basis of past practice, the vacation article had been construed in the past as not allowing such an employee a vacation entitlement. To the arbiter, the vacation contract language appeared clear and so he made the comments below:

> [W]hile evidence of past practice may be admissible to explain an ambiguous provision or to demonstrate that language appearing in the instrument was used in a particular sense different from that which it ordinarily imports, such evidence is wholly inadmissible where the contract language is plain and unambiguous.[1]

Consequently, the arbiter deemed the company's application of the vacation clause in previous years *not* to be decisive in this case in view of the liability imposed for vacation pay by the clear language of the contract.

An interesting dispute developed out of a contract between Bird and Son, Inc., and the United Paper Workers Union. Based on an erroneous interpretation of a contract article, the company had for several years paid double time for certain hours, not so required by the contract, worked by employees. The company contended that the person in the payroll department who made this interpretation was without authority to bind the company, and as soon as it came to the attention of a responsible management member, the past practice was halted. The union, whose members were the beneficiary of this application for several years, alleged that the contract language was indeed ambiguous and that the company's practice revealed and established its true meaning. The company contended that the overtime article of the agreement was clear and unambiguous and insisted it was merely discontinuing a practice which was in contravention of a specific contract clause. It further reminded the arbitrator that under the language of the arbitration clause, he was without power to decide the case on the basis of past practice.

This presented a troublesome dilemma to the arbitrator who, in the opinion of this writer, deftly and wisely tap-danced his way out of the problem. He first concluded that the company had made an erroneous interpretation of the overtime article for several years. The union and the employees had accepted and relied upon that interpretation and therefore had not proposed changes in this particular language when negotiating renewal agreements. Therefore, he commented, "in equity and good conscience, the company should not alter its practice unilaterally but should wait until the contract comes up for renewal and then make the problem a subject matter for collective bargaining." However, the arbitrator, with only the limited powers granted to him by the contract, could only merely interpret and apply the contractual provisions. He had no authority to compel the company to continue to make such payment on equitable grounds. So, under the arbitration clause of the contract, he had to dismiss the grievance and hold that the company did not violate the overtime provision.[2] It is presumed however, that his recommendation to the employer did not fall on closed ears. The case does expose another situation where a clearly established practice was disregarded in the face of unambiguous contract wording.

Similar was the case under another labor agreement but which resulted in a dissimilar arbitral finding. Under a contract providing that employees should be paid only for all work performed on the days indicated on their time reports, an employer was ruled to be entitled to discontinue a past practice of allowing employees to record time for making two setups for a certain production run for which actually only one physical setup was performed. The company argued that its practice was in flat contradiction to the expressed language of the agreement. Ironically, as in the prior case, the only section of the contract that related remotely to the dispute (and which the union relied on) was the provision specifically prohibiting that which the union sought to attain. The union's case in its entirety rested on past practice. The company did not dispute past practice. In the arbitrator's judgment, the company was in no way precluded from changing a practice that was definitely in contravention to the plain meaning and intent of contract wording. Therefore, it could not be argued successfully by the union that a change of practice which in effect brought it into line with contract requirements was at the same time a violation of the contract.[3]

The union was the victor where an employer was held to have violated a contract which provided that seniority and ability should govern in transfers when it refused to transfer female employees to an inspector's job, at the same time transferring junior male employees to it. The fact that it had been a custom to assign such inspecting work to male employees only was immaterial, since the arbiter considered custom *not* controlling where the contract language was clear and he put it in the following way:

> [I]t is well settled both in law and in contract interpretation by arbitrators that custom and practice will be considered as binding and interpretative of contract provisions where there exist ambiguities in the contract, but that a custom and practice cannot prevail where the terms and provisions of an effective agreement are plain and without ambiguities....[4]

The holiday clause from another contract clearly provided that the enumerated holidays would be paid for at straight time rates, when not worked. Accordingly, when a May 30 and July 4 holiday fell on Saturday, and were not worked, but were not paid for by the company, the union filed a grievance demanding payment for same. The company, taken by surprise by this grievance, stated that this language had been in the contract for over six years and that the company had never paid for Saturday holidays. As a matter of fact, in two prior years, holidays fell on Saturdays and the employer did not pay the employees for the holidays and the union raised no objection. The company's defense rested on its practice of not paying for holidays which fell on unworked days. Again, a trio of arbiters presiding over this dispute shot the past practice argument down in flames.

> When disputed contract language is clear and unequivocal, arbitrators have little justification for speculating as to what the intention of the parties might or might not have been when the contract was agreed to ... why Saturday holidays were not paid for in the past in view of this language is difficult to understand, but what the practice of the parties has been cannot control here when the language stating their agreement is beyond dispute.[5]

A different trio of arbitrators in another dispute put it this way:

> While the company argues that the conduct of the parties under this clause supports its view, it has been well-established that an arbitrator cannot rule contrary to the clearly expressed words of the contract.[6]

Arbitrator Charles C. Killingsworth, the impartial umpire under the agreement between Bethlehem Steel Company and the Steelworkers Union, in settling a dispute between these parties expressed his theory as follows:

> [I]n the absence of ambiguity, it is the duty of the umpire to uphold the insistence of one party that a valid agreement be applied exactly as the parties themselves wrote it, even if such strict application results in inconveniences, embarrassment, or even unfairness to the other party to the agreement....

However, this same arbiter in this same case went on to expound on his theory and appeared to allow for the consideration that certain peculiar and compelling circumstances might conceivably have sufficient persuasion to compromise an otherwise definite principle:

> This writer believes that under certain circumstances the past conduct of the parties is a factor that must be given considerable weight in the interpretation of an agreement. This is appropriate, however, only when there is some ambiguity in the agreement, or when both parties to the agreement have actually settled disputes on the basis of a particular interpretation, or in some other way have evinced a positive acceptance or endorsement of that interpretation.[7]

Arbitrator B. Meredith, chairman of a tripartite board in a dispute between Koppers Company, Inc., and the United Mine Workers, District 50, expressed his viewpoint on clear contract language versus conflicting practices and customs.

> Actually, an arbitrator must work on the theory that binding words mean what they say when a new contract has been negotiated and accepted in definite terms, and ordinarily neither party may examine events which occurred prior to the instant contract. This is one way of saying that past practice does not control when the contract language is clear and unambiguous. This being so, it is, therefore, true also that when the language is not clear but is, in fact, ambiguous, the arbitrator must look for help to past precedent and practice.[8]

Arbitrator Edgar L. Warren expressed his opinion on this issue while resolving a grievance between the Lockheed Aircraft Service, Inc., and the Machinists Union:

> Both parties have a right to expect a consistent application of the terms of their agreement, and, generally speaking, practices, as well as arbitrators' decisions, determine what the parties intended when they used particular language. However, if the language of the agreement clearly

and unambiguously indicates that the practices were improper, the arbitrator would have to find that they were in violation of the agreement.[9]

Continuing the debate over the weight and effect to be given a past practice which conflicts with a clearly worded contract provision, another arbitrator expressed his theories as follows:

> The role of usage and custom in connection with the construction or interpretation of written contracts is clear and well-established. The general rule is that usage and custom may be proved in explanation and qualification of the terms of a contract which otherwise would be ambiguous or to demonstrate that the language appearing in the instrument was used in a particular sense different from that which it ordinarily imports, but such evidence is never admitted to make a new contract or to add a new element to one previously made. It may explain any language which is ambiguous but usage or custom cannot vary or contradict what is manifest and plain or be received to give plain and unambiguous language a connotation different from its usual and ordinary import.[10]

This concept was espoused by an arbitrator under a contract which provided for the reinstatement of employees who had been ill if their absence had not exceeded six months' duration. The employer had further conditioned the reinstatement of employees upon a physical fitness certification. This had been its practice for many years and had been well known to the union's officials. The company, of course, argued its right to continue this practice on the basis of a well-established, understood and accepted practice of long duration. However, the language of the agreement pertaining to leaves of absence omitted any mention of such physical fitness requirement in its enunciation of the conditions under which an employee could return to work following such leave. Also, this practice had not been discussed in negotiations. The arbitrator felt that to rule otherwise would require him to enlarge the provisions of this clear and unambiguous sick leave language, and it would have been in direct violation of the collective bargaining agreement. In other words, he would be deciding the issue submitted to him, not exclusively according to the provisions of the sick leave article of the contract, but in accordance with some prior usage or custom not even referred to in this contract article. Accordingly, he ruled that the individual employee involved in this situation which had given rise to the grievance was entitled to return to work after an absence of approximately six months on account of illness, without obtaining a release from the company's medical staff, as had been required by the company.

The above-cited theory seems to be shared by another arbitrator who decided a dispute between National Tube Company and the

Steelworkers Union. In deciding the case where the clear contract language ran afoul of a past practice which seemed to accord with intent, the arbitrator made the following remarks.

> [T]he language, however, is clear. It expresses clearly what the corporation says the parties had in mind. It is almost irrelevant to the union's version to find for the corporation in the matter of intent, in other words, we would merely have to read and apply the language of the agreement to find for the union. We would either have to rewrite that language or disregard it all together.[11]

So stating these alternatives, he had to choose between them. The parties to this contract had given the arbitrator authority only to interpret, apply or determine compliance with the provisions of the contract. Expressly withheld was authority to add to, subtract from or alter in any way such contract clauses. The arbiter went further and remarked that he recognized the dangers that lay in a merely literal, mechanical approach to a contract. However, he considered that an equal problem existed, which had to be avoided—the danger that if he went behind the agreement to discover the parties' intent, he would actually be substituting his own.

Advocating the same philosophy, still another arbitrator viewed it as a legal rule of contract language construction that when contract phrasing is clear and unambiguous, the intent of the parties must be found in its clear wording and not in their conduct, depite the fact that they are supposedly acting properly under its provisions. And, although the parties themselves might possibly act under its terms as they see fit and even contrary to the terms of their contract, this does not justify an arbitrator, at the request of one of the parties, to interpret the agreement otherwise than as written.[12]

Another example of clear and unambiguous contract language versus a conflicting past practice was a case between International Harvester Company and the United Farm Equipment Metal Workers Union. Here, the contractual provision was quite explicit in its requirement that the company furnish the union with seniority lists, and stated precisely what information would be shown on such lists. For several years preceding the current contract, the union had been furnished with seniority lists showing, in addition to the names and clock numbers of employees, their current classifications and dates of hire. The labor agreement, however, in its listing of those items which would be included by the company on a seniority list, did not include employees' job classifications. While there was admittedly no express requirement in the contract for giving employees' classifications on the seniority list, the union, nevertheless, claimed an established practice under that language of including necessary job classifications data on such sheets. The company, on the other hand, denied that the contract obligated it to give classification information on seniority lists. It further asserted that the inclusion of such information in the past was a unilaterally established company practice—not an agreed to interpretation of the contract—which it had a right to discontinue when the contract then in effect expired. So, at the time of entering this new agreement, it had discontinued this practice. The company pointed out that the arbitrator had no authority to compel the inclusion of additional information not specifically detailed by the agreement. The arbitrator made remarks as follows:

> The union's grievance cannot be sustained. The plain fact is that there is no ambiguity in the language of Section 14 and hence it does not require construction ... when contract language is clear and unambiguous, the intent of the parties is to be found in its clear language and not in the parties' conduct, although they are supposedly acting under its terms. To be sure, the parties themselves may, by mutual agreement, act as they see fit under a contract and even contrary to its terms; but this does not justify an arbitrator at the request of one of the parties, in interpreting the contract otherwise than as written.[13]

This is clearly an arbitrator who has adopted the theory that clear contract language is not revised or otherwise changed from its clear meaning by a practice or custom which operates in conflict with such contractual wording. To him, the evidence was plain that the practice of listing the employees' classifications on the seniority roster was established by the company unilaterally. As he remarked, a practice thus established under a prior contract could not be held binding under a new contract that was silent on that subject, in the absence of proof that the practice was continued under the new agreement. This company was obviously careful not to continue this practice into the new agreement.

A comparable problem arose under a contract clause which read as follows:

> Section 11. Employees shall record on a daily time report all work performed on the day indicated on the time report, and no work shall be recorded on any daily time report that was not performed on that day. Where possible, the reports shall indicate the amount of time required to perform each operation listed. There shall be no change made in the employee's daily time report without his knowledge. The daily time report shall be available for employee reference.[14]

No basic disagreement existed as to the former and the current practice on making setups by employees under this contract. For several years, the company had been paying operators for two setups where he was setting up for production runs involving both right- and left-hand parts. An operator would spend the same physical amount of time setting up for a production run of both right- and left-hand parts on a particular item as he would for a run of just left-hand or right-hand parts. However, under the former practice, if the production run was for only right-hand or left-hand parts, the operator was paid for two setups. The company then decided that the practice described was contrary to the contract and employees were advised not to turn in on their time slips for setups not actually performed. Under the new practice, when an operator ran both right- and left-hand parts under the same setup, he was paid only for one setup rather than for two, as was formerly the case. The union, on the other hand, maintained that the prior practice was regarded by both parties as "work performed on the day indicated" within the meaning of Section 11. Therefore, said the union, the company's revised practice constituted an unauthorized reduction in wages contrary to the contract.

After a careful consideration of the factual picture as to the practice here involved, only one conclusion was possible. It was evident from the record that for a number of years employees had been permitted to charge for setup time not actually spent on making setups. Under the company's new practice, they were now paid only for the actual physical setups made. To boil the arbitrator's opinion down to its basic essence, his salient remarks were as follows:

> In order to sustain its case here, the union has to show that the company's current practice for paying on setups constitutes a violation of Section 11 . . . this would involve showing that the operator has been performing work on the day indicated on his time report for which he has not been paid.
> In my judgment, the company is in no way precluded from changing a practice that was definitely in contravention to the plain meaning and intent of Section 11. The first sentence of Section 11 is the only one directly relevant to the instant situation. In the undersigned's judgment, this sentence makes clear beyond question that employees are to record all work performed on any day and that they are not to record any work not performed on any day. . . .
> In other words, the company's past practice which has been discontinued and which the union seeks to have restored was in my judgment contrary to both the letter and the spirit of Section 11. Therefore, it cannot be argued successfully that a change of practice which in effect springs it into line with contract requirements, is at the same time a violation of contract.[15]

Arbitrator Jean T. McKelvey found herself between two adversaries, the Sterilon Corporation and the United Rubber Workers Union, over the employer's creation of seniority to employees transferred from the bargaining unit to supervisory positions. McKelvey endorsed the same principles as have been heretofore espoused:

> In interpreting a contract, arbitrators look first to the language of the agreement. If the language is unclear or ambiguous, they search for the intent of the parties at the time the agreement was written. If intent could not be ascertained, they look to past practice and precedent as guides to interpretation. . . . Inasmuch as the contract so clearly answers the first question posed in this submission, it is not necessary for the arbitrator to consider either intent or past practice. . . .[16]

Arbitrator Hyman Parker, appointed under the rules of the American Arbitration Association to settle a contract difference between McLouth Steel Corporation and the Steelworkers Union, had the following to say on the subject:

> Past practice which has developed by agreement, acquiescence or mutual acceptability is often helpful, if not decisive, in determining the intent of the parties, where the provisions of an agreement are ambiguous and reasonably susceptible of several interpretations. In such a case, the parties themselves have given the stamp of approval to a certain interpretation by their mutually accepted practice. This general rule, however, *does not ordinarily apply* if the agreement is clear and unambiguous so that the intent of the parties is mandatory from the language used.
>
> While the parties themselves may by mutual agreement or conduct deviate from the agreement, or engage in a course of action which is contrary to its provisions, an arbitrator, however, is bound to interpret and apply the agreement as it is written . . . under the circumstances, the past practice (in this case) must be subordinated to what, in my opinion, are the clear provisions of the agreement.[17]

A Variant Viewpoint

As stated earlier, decisions which express principles like those detailed above are numerous in published arbitration reports. The above few are a mere sampling of what must be admitted to be the arbitral opinion of the majority who decide such matters. But also as mentioned before, although they are fewer in number, there is still a strong voice representing another viewpoint. In view of who it is among professional arbitrators who speak to the contrary, their viewpoint must be considered to carry substantial import. As promised, the following are a few illustrations of such contrary holdings. One of the more eloquent spokesmen in the arbitration process and an arbiter who has sometimes found past practice and custom to be more purposeful than the wording of the agreement, which presumably expressed the desires and intentions of the parties, is Peter Seitz. Several of his arbitral opinions have so expressed that a possibility exists for such a holding under the right set of circumstances. Typical of these is found in the eloquence of his remarks while resolving a dispute between the *Cleveland Press* and *Plain Dealer* and the Cleveland Newspaper Guild:

> The art of contract interpretation (as subtle and as mysterious an art as exists!) involves a search for what each party has a reasonable basis to expect of the other in consequence of the consummation of a metaphysical thing we call "Agreement." There is general consensus that the best evidence of their "Agreement" (their mutual undertakings, their joint will, their bargain), by far, is the word in the writing they solemnly signed. Labor-Management Arbitrators *have not regarded themselves to have been imprisoned by the word expressed in the printed booklet constituting a copy of the "contract," and, in appropriate cases, have put aside the parol evidence rule* to admit and consider side agreements, statements made at negotiations and other alleged proofs of the true substance of the "Agreement." Probably the most frequently urged basis for a departure from the safe and secure harborage of the expressed words of the writing is the existence of an established and accepted practice, custom or usage. *The arbitration reports are replete with instances wherein arbitrators have been persuaded, by either employers or unions, to cast off the mooring lines of the written document and to beat into the hazardous waters of "practice." This is as it should be,* because it is well within the traditions of our legal system, in the course of contract construction, for adjudicators (courts and arbitrators) to conclude that the actions, conduct, behavior, et cetera, of the parties, over time, have more eloquently manifested and demonstrated what the true bargain of the parties had been than the too general or ambiguous language which they had placed in the document.[18]

Because arbiter Seitz alludes to the parol evidence rule, it is probably in order to provide a few words of explanation in this connection. This is basically an evidential rule pertaining to extrinsic evidence. It primarily operates to exclude all evidence of prior or contemporaneous oral understandings which are offered by one party or the other to alter the effect of a written contract. It may be presented to an arbitrator by one party or the other with the contention that the written agreement as agreed upon between the parties was not intended to represent as literal or effective an understanding as some oral or unwritten understanding. Most arbitrators receive such evidence where the party introducing it is attempting, through its usage, to establish a mutual interpretation or practice under the contract to be relied upon to give meaning to contract terms. However, it further holds that a clear and definite meaning of a contract should not be held to give way to oral testimony. Also, any ambiguity of wording making it susceptible to more than one interpretation may be resolved by the oral testimony of mutual interpretation or practice understood and substantially accepted by the other party.

Under an agreement between Nicolet Industries, Inc., and the Textile Workers Union, a recognition clause which had been contained within the agreement for over 19 years clearly provided that a truck driver classification was embraced by the contract. Despite this clear wording, the parties had operated as though the truck driver was outside the bargaining unit. Over the years, his wage schedule did not conform to the agreement and his union dues were not deducted in accordance with that contractual provision. Then, the union decided to seek through arbitration jurisdiction over this classification. Arbitrator Eli Rock decided the controversy and reached the following conclusion:

> The language of the recognition clause cannot, it seems to this arbitrator, offset this contrary, actual fact of the case. Obviously, the parties have had a full understanding, the clear framework of which cannot be disputed in any significant measure, to the effect that the driver was not in the unit. There can be no room left for doubt that this *was* their mutual agreement. How then, can it logically be contended that because of a broad and general definition of the bargaining unit, which failed specifically to exclude this final employee, the parties should not be regarded as having intended otherwise.[19]

Arbitrator Edgar A. Jones, Jr., ruled that an employer violated its labor agreement when it unilaterally stopped paying chief stewards for time spent at arbitration hearings in which they were not witnesses. The parties' consistent practice for a considerable period of time had been to pay chief stewards for such time. Significant to arbitrator Jones was that the parties here had jointly interpreted the language of the agreement over a significant period of time to allow compensation of the chief steward from the plant building where the grievance arose for his presence at the hearing, irrespective of whether he was a witness. His comments, relevant to our examination here, were as follows:

> Even language which by its clear terms brooks no interpretation but one can be effectively amended, even repealed, by a course of contrary interpretation indulged by the Parties over a significant period of time. The actions of the parties subsequent to the execution of the Agreement are often far more revealing of consensual intent than are quite explicit but inactivated contract terms. The reason is obvious. Labor-management agreements do not become static memorials once reduced to writing. They are an important part, but nonetheless only a part, of the active process of effectuating a constructive workable relationship among the parties.[20]

In addition to these interesting remarks of arbitrator Jones were his remarks regarding agreements which contained or were minus a past practice clause. On this point, he remarked that some contracts contain a provision indicating the intent of the parties to limit the accretion of past practices to the term of the instant contract. He further stated that the effect of that type of provision is that a past practice established prior to the execution of the current agreement containing the limiting provision simply dies unless it is either embodied in terms in the new agreement or is once again adhered to in practice after the execution of the new contract. The agreement in dispute here did not contain any clause which could be properly construed as terminative of past practice.

This same arbiter was selected by Bonanza Airlines, Inc., and the International Brotherhood of Teamsters to rule on a very unique issue. The employees of the airlines had formerly been represented by the Machinists Union, but the Teamsters succeeded the Machinists by winning a representational election. Under the agreement with the Machinists Union, the employer had a long-standing practice of paying employees who worked overtime on their day off on the basis of a shift differential of the shift that worked, rather than on the basis of the differential of the shift to which they were regularly assigned. The applicable contract had been in effect for almost 10 years and this practice, now challenged by the Teamsters union, had been consistently followed throughout that period without any protest from the predecessor union that had originally negotiated the language. The Teamsters union, which took over the contract and the bargaining rights from the predecessor union, argued that it should not be bound by any change from the expressed terms of the agreement which had been acquiesced to by the prior union. Holding that the employer could continue its well-established practice despite specific contract language, the arbitrator explained his conclusions in the following manner.

> In this case, the company's practice of computing shift differential for overtime purposes extended over a number of years, and involved a sufficiently large number of employees as to compel the conclusion that the predecessor union must be taken to have been aware of it. When the Teamsters acquired the bargaining rights previously exercised by the Machinists, it took this Agreement as thus interpreted by the employer and the Machinists over the years. The "agreement" had become its express language plus (or minus) the mutual administrative conduct of the parties which is called "past practice" (there being no contractual provision excluding such a conclusion). That being so, these grievances are not well taken, and must be denied, irrespective of any element of timeliness, which by 1964 had become embodied in the Agreement as allowable for the employer.[21]

Usually, the right of the employer to unilaterally establish reasonable rules covering employee conduct and behavior is an accepted condition between the parties. The contract between West Virginia Pulp and Paper Company and the United Paper Makers and Paper Workers Union provided that "the company shall regulate and prescribe all other working conditions and conditions of employment and operation that do not violate the terms of this agreement." However, this clear management prerogative had been compromised over a period of 13 years by the company in not establishing such rules unilaterally, but instead negotiating them with the union. Finally, when the employer attempted to act unilaterally in accord with the contract, the union protested. Upholding the grievance, arbitrator David A. Wolff made the following remarks:

> In the opinion of this arbitrator, the situation is most unusual, if not unique. The parties have provided that the company shall regulate and prescribe working conditions and conditions of employment and operations that do not violate the terms of the agreement. However, in fact and as shown, since their first agreement in 1946 and up to the issuance of the company of its here challenged October 1959 rules, the parties have always negotiated on the inclusion or exclusion of such rules as a matter of course.

Making this determination, arbitrator Wolff concluded that the employer's right of "unilateral action" had been made "extremely limited" by the past practice.[22]

Another unique situation developed where a labor agreement contained a clear provision requiring pay to employees for all legal holidays. Despite this language, the employer had never paid for Good Friday, one of the legal holidays in that state. Arbitrator C.F. Mugridge, when examining the relevant evidence at the hearing, was provided with substantial evidence that the union had traded away its Good Friday pay demand for certain other considerations during negotiations. However, for whatever reasons, the company and the union did not so express their agreement in explicit contract wording. Therefore, the practice under their agreement was contradictory to this plain contract language and it was this practice which Mr. Mugridge ruled was binding, not the contract.[23]

Arbitrator Lewis M. Gill was another arbiter of established stature who ruled that clear contract language was not the true indicator of the parties' intentions. The following is what he said in deciding a dispute between Linear, Inc., and the United Rubber Workers Union:

> In general, I am personally inclined to the view that the contract language should govern, if it is absolutely clear and unambiguous, despite a showing of practice to the contrary. What we have here, however, is something more than just a practice of the parties. The uncontradicted evidence shows that at the time the provision in question was negotiated, there was a specific assurance by the company negotiators that it would be interpreted and applied in the manner now urged by the union. The ensuing practice of applying it in that way, in the press room, merely carried out that commitment.[24]

Again, we return to arbitrator Peter Seitz. For many years, it had been a practice to require clerks to perform clean-up operations at the end of their work day and to pay them no extra compensation for up to ten minutes of such work. However, when they worked beyond this for 11 to 15 minutes, their compensation was at straight time for the quarter-hour. There was a clear contract provision requiring that any work in excess of eight hours per day would be compensated at time and one-half overtime premium. But, under the company's past practices, such employees received this contractual guarantee only if they worked more than 15 minutes. Finally, after many years under this practice, the union protested by grievance, demanding that the clear contract language be applied and employees be paid time and one-half commencing with the first minute of overtime. Their entire case was based on the "crystal clear and unambiguous" contract wording. Arbitrator Seitz felt differently.

> The written contract is, of course, the strongest kind of evidence of what the parties willed, intended or agreed upon. *An arbitrator will not ordinarily look beyond its unambiguous language.* Where, *however,* as here, *the parties have unmistakably demonstrated how they themselves have read and regarded the meaning* and force of the language, and where *the meaning varies from its normal intendment,* the arbitrator *should not,* indeed, *cannot* close his eyes to this demonstration....[25] [Emphasis added.]

Thus rejecting the union's arguments, the grievance was denied. However, he did indicate that his ruling extended only to a continuation of the practice when the employer had a legitimate need for clean-up work. It was not a broad and general ruling that could be utilized by the employer to expect employees to work beyond eight hours for brief periods without the contractual extra compensation.

Similarly, arbitrator Joseph Sherbow accorded with this viewpoint when he ruled that an employer was not violating a contract requiring that it pay to the union's social security fund a sum equal to 3 percent of the employees' gross wages, when it first indicated an amount equal to one-third of the gross wages. This was the amount employees charged off, for income tax purposes, as expenses for using their own cars and for other expenses on their jobs; for this reason, the employer paid only 3 percent of the balance. Although the contract wording seemed clear and specific to the arbiter, the facts that (1) the union had accepted such payments for several years without protest; and (2) other employers with whom the union had contracts containing the same language had followed a similar procedure, indicated that it was the understanding of the parties that the amount representing expenses would be deducted from gross wages before computing the 3 percent payment.[26]

It is quite apparent that the generalization used by many arbitrators that such decisions have formulated a "well-established principle" is closer to being an erroneous generalization than an established doctrine. Why is it that employers as organizations, and unions as institutions, do not, one or the other, get more aroused over such disparate arbitral conclusions? Perhaps an explanation is not so hard to find. When some arbitrators decide cases involving subcontracting disputes, they rule that some contractual clauses (the recognition article, the listing of job classifications, etc.) contain implied restrictions on managerial discretion over this vital area. To most employers, such arbitrators who rule accordingly are to be avoided if possible. This is an example of arbitral opinion which arouses employers universally. On the other hand, those arbitrators who rule that management has few limitations upon its managerial discretion to subcontract, where the labor agreement is silent on the subject, universally cause unions to be apprehensive of their services.

But when arbitral opinion such as that reviewed in this chapter is issued, only the losing party in that particular dispute is actually provoked. The rest of the industrial community, both employers and unions, do not become uneasy. The reason for this is simple. Both parties realize that in any given case, either side may find itself (1) arguing for or against a past practice or clear contract wording; or (2) contending for a particular interpretation for an ambiguous contract provision supported by some particular practice. For this reason, it is not uncommon to find two particular parties at an arbitration table with one arguing that the clear language should be set aside in favor of compelling practice, after an arbitration hearing in which this same party argued that the clear language of another provision must prevail and an established but contradictory practice be ignored. This is merely one of the factors which makes past practice the no man's land of the collective bargaining agreement.

3. Benefit Versus Gratuity

An employer may hang himself by his own petard by his benevolent gesture in voluntarily and unilaterally granting to employees additional material considerations not required by the labor agreement. Although his initial motivations may be of the highest order, an employer may find himself bound to continue such additional material considerations when one day he decides to discontinue them. This is a regrettable fact of industrial life. Once an employer is bound by the terms of a collective bargaining agreement, he may find himself unable to extricate himself from a previously established gratuitous act, although his reasons for wanting to do so may be quite valid and substantial. Many an organized employer has elected to provide his employees with an extracontractual consideration, merely as a good faith employee relations action. There are many others who have put forth such gratuities during periods when their employees were not yet represented by a labor organization. In either case, such employers have, more often than not, found themselves obliged to continue the gratuity against their preference—and perhaps despite the fact they did not intend to halt it permanently. Such extracontractual considerations take many forms, but most often express themselves in terms of a Christmas bonus or turkey or gift, but they can also be in the form of additional wash-up time or rest periods, discounts on employee-purchased items, and the like. Such extra allowances may ultimately be construed by an arbitrator as having taken the form of a benefit or a working condition without change or interruption.

Many employers might, under more favorable circumstances, be inclined to consider issuance or granting of extracontractual arrangements and considerations, if it were not for this inherent danger. For this reason, many employers think twice, and then a third time, before commencing some additional material consideration. They realize that once they start, they may forfeit their right to make any unilateral change in that which they unilaterally and voluntarily started.

Some eminent arbitrators have espoused what may be properly considered the prevailing viewpoint. Archibald Cox and John T. Dunlop have made the following remarks:

A collective bargaining agreement should be deemed, unless a contrary
condition is manifest, to carry forward for its term the major terms and
conditions of its employment, not covered by the agreement, which
prevail when the agreement was executed.[1]

Whatever meaning is assigned to the phrase "the major terms
and conditions of employment" is an interesting variable from one arbitrator to another. The logic of the proposition put forth by Cox and
Dunlop would make such extracontractual considerations a part of the
complete agreement, and therefore not subject to unilateral discontinuance.

The National Labor Relations Board

There is another reason why employers are always anxious about
their right to discontinue such practices—that is, the well-founded fear
that such action might be found to be an unfair labor practice if its union
pursued the matter under the National Labor Relations Act. It has been
held by the National Labor Relations Board that an employer's
unilateral action to change some element of benefit or compensation,
when it isn't mentioned in the contract, and has not been discussed in
contract negotiations, constitutes the unfair practice of refusing to
bargain. An extraordinary example of this occurred at the Westinghouse
Electric Corporation complex of plants located in the Baltimore area.
Cafeteria facilities servicing these plants were operated by an independent catering company under contract with Westinghouse. Pursuant to
the contract, the caterer paid Westinghouse a rental of $1.00 per year and
Westinghouse provided the capital equipment necessary to operate the
facilities. The relevant portion of this contract with the caterer provided:
"The quality and prices of the meals served, and the hours of service
thereof, in said cafeterias shall at all times be reasonable."

About 45 percent of Westinghouse employees ate lunches at the
cafeterias. The majority of employees carried their own lunches, sup-
plementing them with beverages obtained from vending machines. Then
the caterer announced that it intended to increase cafeteria food prices,
and posted notices of an increase of five cents in the price of hot food
on trays and an increase of one cent in the price of carry-out coffee.
Thereafter, one of the unions representing Westinghouse employees
sought to meet with the company to discuss these price increases.
Westinghouse arranged for meetings of the union with the caterer in the
offices of the company, but took the position that although its representatives were present, it could not discuss these matters or bargain

concerning them with the union because it had no power to fix or control the prices of food items served in the cafeterias by the caterer. The union then filed a charge with the NLRB. The three majority Board members based their decision, supporting the union's claim, on the fact that Westinghouse supplied the cafeteria in order to attract employees who otherwise would not have accepted employment there if eating facilities were not provided. They also held that the cafeteria prices were, under the circumstances of this case, "conditions of employment" within the statutory meaning of these words as used in the Act, and a mandatory subject of bargaining between the plant owner and one of the plant unions. The Board was apparently unwilling to acknowledge that in determining whether a given matter should be deemed a mandatory bargaining subject, the courts, as well as the Board itself, had previously recognized a legal distinction between those subjects which have a material or significant impact upon wages, hours, or other conditions of employment, and those which are only indirectly, incidentally, or remotely related to those subjects.

Fortunately from Westinghouse's point of view, it did not rest satisfied with the Board's decision and so appealed it to the Fourth Circuit Court of Appeals. This court, in a rehearing of the matter before Chief Judge Haynesworth (whose appointment to the United States Supreme Court was later rejected) overturned the Board's ruling. Significant to the court's reversal of the Board decision was the fact that the caterer, not Westinghouse, determined the prices of the food and coffee served in the cafeterias. They rejected the Board's conclusion that employees who bought lunches at the cafeterias would quit good jobs at high pay if they had to bring their own lunches as being only a presumption, unsupported by any evidence. The Board had made the following remarks:

> If it did not have these facilities, it would not be able to attract the necessary number of employees to man its plants. In practical terms, on-site eating facilities are held out to the employees and prospective employees as an inducement to work for Westinghouse. They are thus conditions of employment. The problem is as simple as that.[2]

The Court, on the other hand, could not find one word of testimony to support this conclusion that the employer would have been unable to attract the necessary number of employees to man its plants if it did not provide cafeteria space. Secondly, no testimony supported any conclusion that on-site eating facilities were portrayed as an inducement to work for Westinghouse. The Court went on to say:

> Stripped of unsupported presumptions and guesses, the statement of the Board majority is that anyone who prefers buying his meals in a

cafeteria to bringing his lunch from home is, for that reason, a captive customer of the cafeteria. The only compulsion is the individual's own desire or preference, which is precisely the same as saying that there is no compulsion. If the plant were entirely surrounded by restaurants, the same individual might prefer eating in the cafeteria, which, under the Board's reasoning, would make him a "captive customer." No one testified that it was impossible or even inconvenient for an employee to bring his lunch from home if he decided not to buy his lunch or coffee at the cafeteria. Thousands do exactly that without any loss of time, loss of wages, disciplinary action, or any other ill effect.

The Board would order Westinghouse to bargain with (union) about prices charged by the independent caterer with full knowledge that Westinghouse cannot make any enforceable contract to change those prices since it does not set them. This Court long since decided that the purpose of collective bargaining is to produce an agreement and not merely to engage in talk for the sake of going through the motions. The Board calls upon Westinghouse to here engage in that very form of fictional bargaining condemned in the Highland Park Case.

In view of the majority of this Court, it was not the intent of Congress in enacting the National Labor Relations Act to sweep every act by every employer within the ambit of "conditions of employment."[3]

The outcome of this case was a fortunate one for this particular employer. However, this does not indicate that any other employer might fare as well. It is an interesting examination because it wholly reveals the type of reasoning an employer may encounter in cases of this type before the NLRB. And, if the employer's geographical location places him before an appellate court other than the Fourth Circuit, there is always some degree of uncertainty as to the ultimate outcome of any appeal he might make of a Board decision. The Westinghouse case dramatically portrays the dilemma of the employer who has gratuitously provided some condition or arrangement convenient to his employees, which may ultimately be ruled, in some forum of adjudication, as a binding condition of employment to which his employees are entitled and over which he has lost unilateral control.

Disputes over an employer's nonpayment of a Christmas bonus have also gone before the National Labor Relations Board for review. In one such situation, the company had given a cash bonus to all employees at its plant each year for the period from 1956 to 1964. In May 1965, a majority of employees selected a union as their bargaining representative and a contract was executed in September of that year. No mention was made of a Christmas bonus during contract negotiations and no provision therefore was included in the contract. The union filed its complaint with the Board, alleging that the employer violated the Labor-Management Relations Act (LMRA) by its unilaterally withholding the Christmas bonus. The employer argued that no provision for a

Christmas bonus was included in the contract and, therefore, it was not obligated to bargain on it. Secondly, the employer claimed that the union had waived its rights of negotiation since it had proposed during negotiations that existing practices be continued but such a provision was not included in the contract. Third, it contended that the union had not exhausted the grievance procedures of the contract with regard to the employer's failure to pay the bonuses. The Board did not agree. To them, the silence of the contract on the subject did not constitute a relinquishment by the union of its statutory right to bargain about employment conditions for employees. It found significant the fact that during contract negotiations the subject of a Christmas bonus was never discussed. Therefore, to them, its exclusion from the contract did not mean that the union waived its right to bargain on the issue when the employer changed its prior practices. Somehow, another salient fact escaped them: During collective bargaining the union had proposed a contract provision stating that all existing practices be continued, but no such provision was included among the final contract terms.[4]

Another case on Christmas bonuses which came before the Board produced an even more startling outcome when its fact situation is carefully considered. Here, the employer for many years had negotiated contracts with eight unions, including the four unions bringing charges with the Board. None of the contracts with any of the unions had even referred to, much less provided for, the Christmas bonus which the employer had initiated and had been paying for the prior 20 years. In each instance, the employer decided in late November or early December to pay the bonus on a selected payroll date just before Christmas. Beginning in 1961, six years before these union charges were brought, the bonus had been paid by a separate check, accompanied by a company letter expressing seasons greetings and stressing that the bonus was "*voluntary.*" Without consulting the unions, management had always determined who the beneficiaries would be and what amounts would be paid. Until Christmas 1965, the full bonus of an employee had been the equivalent to two weeks of pay, at the wage rate actually being paid to him on the distribution date. In 1965, however, the bonus amounted to two weeks' pay at the employees' actual December 1963 and 1964 pay rates and thus fell short of two weeks' *current* pay.

Each of the unions protested this unilateral departure from practice. The company then met with each union contending that the bonus was "a voluntary thing" and refused to discuss determining an amount.

Significant, at least from the company's point of view, was the fact that in the 1962 and 1964 contracts, the unions accepted "zipper" clauses, which provided that "this contract is complete in itself" and "sets forth all the terms and conditions of the agreement between the parties." No mention was made of the Christmas bonus in negotiating these zipper clauses except in the negotiations of one of the agreements. This particular union agreed to the clause only after the employer gave his assurance that he had no idea of "the bonus being stopped or being altered." No such discussions were held in the negotiations with the other seven unions.

Despite all these facts (and a bargaining history which showed that in 1962 the union attempted to secure a contractual Christmas bonus payment and failed), the Board ordered the employer to cease and desist from refusing to bargain concerning payment of the Christmas bonus and unilaterally altering the formula for bonus payment. Board member Zagoria, dissenting, exhaled the only breath of fresh air surrounding this case. He recognized the pertinent factors which should have produced a contrary decision. None of the eight contracts governed the payment of the bonus. Furthermore, each time the bonus was paid, it was accompanied with a letter indicating its voluntary nature. It was conceded no antiunion motivation was involved in the change in method of computation; rather, the record demonstrated the employer's decision was based solely upon economic considerations.[5]

The Board ruled that another employer violated the LMRA by discontinuing its past practice with respect to payments of year-end Christmas bonuses to employees in the bargaining unit, without notifying and consulting with the certified union. The employer principally contended that the Christmas bonus fell outside the area of compulsory collective bargaining, since the bonuses were gratuities, not wages. Alternatively, the company asserted that the union waived its right with respect to the bonus and that the union made no prior demand to bargain concerning the subject. For a period of at least 11 years, virtually all persons in the plant annually received a Christmas bonus. This practice was discontinued in December of a year in which the labor agreement had been entered in February. The contract contained no reference to bonuses inasmuch as that subject was not raised or discussed. The trial examiner's holding, later supported by the Board, concluded that the bonuses were a formal, regular part of that unit employee's wage structure and constituted a term or condition of employment as to which the company was obligated to bargain with the union.

This is a fascinating concept when applied to this case, since the employer had never refused to bargain with the union on the subject during contract negotiations. Secondly, the Board concluded that the subject of bonuses had not been "consciously explored" by the parties during the contract negotiations and, therefore, there was no claim and unmistakable waiver of interest on the matter by the union; and, further, that the union had no statutory obligation to initiate bargaining with respect to the bonuses. This is an even more fascinating concept. In substance, the Board's theory was that the union had not defaulted on its opportunity to bargain on this matter by its failure to do so during negotiations. And further, the union was under no obligation to raise the matter. Presumably, when the two parties sit at the bargaining table, it is the expectation of the employer that the union will raise for discussion any and all subjects it deems appropriate to bargaining. The employer also expects that if the union wants to obtain new or improved wages, benefits or conditions, or preserve the maintenance and continuation of those then possessed, it will present proposals and demands for negotiation. Clearly, the Board does not view this approach, which is understood and accepted by both parties at the bargaining table, to be the one appropriate to their interests. Evidently, the consummation of a labor agreement concludes nothing except negotiations on those matters expressly covered by written provisions of the agreement, and nothing prevents the union from raising new or additional subjects for bargaining not covered by some written provision. In any case, such was the outcome in this Board matter.[6]

This next Board case may provide some hope for employers that the rationale may be mellowing on this subject. The case referred to dealt with a Christmas bonus which an employer had paid to its employees each year since 1947. However, when, 20 years later in 1967, it experienced a net loss for the first time, it wrote to the union advising it of this general economic condition. Late in that same year, negotiations began for a new contract. Among other subjects covered by the employer's letter to the union was a statement that the Christmas bonus would be given in 1967 but that "next year there would be no Christmas bonus unless there was a profit." During negotiations, the union examined the company's books since the employer's financial condition was a factor in the bargaining for a new contract. In one of the bargaining sessions in March, a union representative commented that he presumed the Christmas bonus would not be given because of the company's financial situation. The company's representative replied that the bonus would not be paid "if financial conditions continue as they had been." When the employer showed a net loss for the year 1968, it gave no bonus. Upon the company's failure to pay the bonus, the union filed a refusal to bargain charge with the Board. Fortunately for the employer, the Board held that the union had been afforded every opportunity to bargain about the elimination of the Christmas bonus during lengthy contract negotiations, and it simply failed to do so. The union could not allege that it was not aware of the company's intention not to pay the 1968 bonus unless there was a profit. Further, the Board pointed out that the union had adequate opportunity to determine whether a profit was being made. Solely for these reasons, the Board found that the employer did not violate Section 8 (a) (5) and (1) of the Act by unilaterally eliminating the 1968 bonus.[7]

We turn now to those arbital decisionmakers whose opinions are of primary concern for this book. W. Willard Wirtz once upheld a grievance on the company's discontinuance of the five-minute wash-up period before lunch and at the end of the shift as arbitrable despite the absence of any contract reference to wash-up time. Significant in the light of this ruling was the fact that the contract was silent and also defined an arbitrable grievance as one involving a claimed violation of the contract, or a failure to fulfill a contract obligation. In addition to those factors, the contract further stated that "the parties have set forth herein all the agreements between them with respect to wages, hours, and other conditions of employment." Despite these elements which must be presumed as having some relevancy, arbitrator Wirtz expressed his viewpoint of the principles as follows:

> There is also a fast growing body of private *arbitration precedent which denies any broad managerial right, in the absence of express reservation, to change important practices during the contract term.* There is sound basis for this increasingly recognized principle of industrial relationship. It contributes to the stability of the contract relationship and to keeping at a minimum disruptions of production by resort to economic force. It conforms with broad principles of reasonableness and fairness which suggest that the usual explanation for not mentioning a particular established practice in the contract is that everybody assumes it has become a part of the accepted situation. A perhaps even more practical consideration is that any other rule would lead to an unfortunate cluttering up of the contract with a loss of detailed references to existing practices.[8]

This rationale comports with the majority prevailing arbitral view of this matter. However, as we shall learn in Chapter 4, there is a strong wind of arbitral opinion blowing in favor of the preservation of certain managerial prerogatives when challenged by past practice.

Benefits in Arbitration

The term benefits as used here could be synonymous with working conditions and is intended to embrace such matters as wash-up periods, lunch-period arrangements, vacation pay, holidays, leaves of absence, severance pay, jury duty pay, and the like. Such coverage is intended to differentiate from gratuity disputes which are subsequently covered herein.

RULINGS IN FAVOR OF THE EMPLOYER

The International Association of Machinists claimed as established privilege the right to use of personal radios by employees in a new jet aircraft repair facility at Eastern Airlines. Under the contract between the parties, it stated that "any privileges now enjoyed by the employees such as daily rest periods, etc., will be maintained unless those privileges are abused." Arbitrator Lewis Yagoda concluded that the practice of using personal radios in the plant did not show an unbroken, undeviating, mutually consistent administration which was necessary to establish it as a continuing privilege. It appeared that the practice existed only subject to management permission, modification, or prohibition, and that permission had always been required for the use of radios by employees. Secondly, their use had been restricted as to the place and the programs, and management permission to bring in radios for the World Series was the single instance to which the union could point where management had specifically permitted radios in the jet repair facility.[9]

The United Steelworkers Union had a contract with the National Tube Co. which required the continuance of "practices relating to hours, overtime, or scheduling heretofore in effect." The union's grievance dealt with a claim that a sole male tabulating clerk be allowed to eat his lunch on the job, with a paid lunch period, based on an alleged prior practice of the employer. The arbiter found the union's claim of past practice too sparse and too inconsistent to constitute a binding pattern which management was compelled to follow. Only four male employees had received a paid lunch period on 26 occasions over a two-year period. There were occasions when male employees working in this department received a half-hour unpaid lunch period and on all occasions, all female tabulating clerks had been provided with a thirty-minute unpaid period.[10]

In a vacation pay dispute, a contract between G.F. Zeller's Sons, Inc., and the International Fur and Leather Workers Union provided vacations with pay for employees who had completed one or more years of service between June and October, but did not specify the amount of service required during the preceding year to qualify for a full vacation. So, the employer did not award a full vacation allotment to employees who were permanently laid off shortly before the vacation season. It was held that such employees were not entitled to full vacation pay, but merely pro rata vacation pay. Since this particular situation was not foreseen by the parties, such interpretation was applied by the arbiter since in the past, when employees were laid off, they made up their lost time between June 1 and October 1 in order to qualify for the vacation.

Therefore, if the time worked during a given year had no bearing on whether an employee was entitled to his vacation, as contended by the union, such a practice would obviously not have been followed. To resolve the issue, therefore, the arbiter turned to logic and equity for a guidepost—this proved to be a pro-rated vacation payment award.[11]

A company-paid clothing allowance which would be applicable to 70 employees was the issue in a contract dispute between the Purex Corporation and the UAW. The labor agreement stated that the company would pay each employee $1.25 monthly "as a clothing allowance which amount it is agreed will compensate employees for the excessive or abnormal wear due to the nature of the product being handled." Employees in some departments of the plant had received the clothing allowance for several years by virtue of this contractual provision. However, employees in the plastic department from which the grievance originated had never been paid such an allowance. Three years after the establishment of the plastic department, this grievance was filed by an individual in the quality control classification. The parties agreed that the disposition of this grievance would govern the disposition of similar pending grievances of the other 70 plastic department employees. The past practice of several years' duration also was of sufficient repetition to justify a conclusion that the parties had, by virtue of that practice, attributed a meaning to this contract wording and had resolved any ambiguities that might have been considered as lurking within its terminology. Secondly, the evidence concerning negotiations clearly favored the company's interpretation. Lastly, the union's evidence was insufficient to establish that the grievant's clothing, much less the clothing of the other 69 employees in the department, suffered "excessive or abnormal wear due to the nature of the product being handled."[12]

Another dispute centered around a union claim that employees were entitled to be paid by the company for time spent obtaining medical care on days subsequent to the day on which their occupational injury occurred. A contractual provision allowed for payment by the company for time spent receiving medical care on the day of the injury, and for the balance of that day if the employee was sent home. When the union failed to present adequate evidence to prove an established practice of permitting employees to obtain medical care on company-paid time, subsequent to the day on which the injury occurred, the arbitrator found the contractual language to be both limiting and controlling.[13]

As mentioned earlier, Christmas bonuses and annual gifts of one type or another, and their preservation or discontinuance, are often subjects of arbitral disputes between the parties. Arbitrator Clair V. Duff was called upon to resolve one such grievance arising between the Rockwell-Standard Corporation and the United Steelworkers Union.

The history of the company's gift contributions to its employees in this case makes an interesting study.

For several years, the company distributed Christmas baskets to all employees. During the depression years of the thirties, the company discontinued all Christmas distributions. In 1935, the company sponsored a party and distributed cash bonuses equivalent to one or two weeks' pay. In 1936, a cash Christmas bonus was paid, and, in addition, Christmas baskets including turkey and groceries were distributed to all employees. No bonuses were distributed in 1937, 1938, or 1939 because of the company's depressed financial condition. However, again in 1940, the company distributed a cash Christmas bonus. This practice continued for the next five years until the unit was organized by the Steelworkers. During negotiations, which culminated in an initial agreement, the union requested that the contract include a provision continuing the payment of Christmas cash bonuses. The company refused to agree to a contract provision, contending that such bonuses were intended as gifts. For the next several years, the company authorized and paid bonuses as it had in previous years. However, in 1954, the company made a minor change in its pattern of bonus calculations by awarding employees with less than one year's service a pro-rated bonus based on 40 hours at their regular rate of pay, as determined by their months of service. The union filed a grievance contesting this change in calculation, but the company maintained that the Christmas bonus was a gift and persisted in its refusal to alter its method of payment.

Following these arguments, the company posted the following bulletin board notice to all employees.

> In reply to a request by a number of employees regarding the policy of distribution of Turkeys at Thanksgiving time and Christmas and the payment of a year end cash bonus, the management will make every effort to post notices on the bulletin boards of the various buildings within a reasonable period of time prior to distribution or payment dates.
>
> The management as in the past retains the discretionary rights to decide if Turkeys will be distributed and if a year end cash bonus will be paid, and what method of calculation will be used.
>
> It is our earnest desire to continue our policy of many years but it only is possible when operations remain productive and profitable.

In December of that same year, the company again paid the year-end bonus. Again in the contract negotiations, which occurred in the next year, the union repeated its request for contractual coverage for the bonus, and the company persisted with its prior position on the matter. However, the union did not acquiesce in the company's position but insisted that continuance of the bonus was protected by the "prior agreements" clause of the contract.

In that same year and in the next year, the company again authorized and paid the year-end checks, but in the next subsequent year, it advised the employees that business conditions dictated that it was necessary to reduce the year-end bonus to amounts less than had formerly been paid. This was done in November and the union instantly grieved the company's announcement. While the grievance was in process, and prior to the case arriving in arbitration, the company made the payments to the employees on the reduced basis. The union relied principally on the argument that a past practice existed that year-end bonuses would be paid. Significant to the arbiter's denial of the union's claim was the fact that (1) the past practice had been not to pay the bonus when the employer was not in a financial position to do so; (2) the company's statements to its employees always had emphasized that the bonus was a voluntary gift and not a part of any wage expectancy; and (3) the parties had bargained on the issue during negotiations and the union had been unable to persuade the company to include a specific contractual provision covering the matter.

In determining whether the Christmas bonus was a gift or part of the employee's wages, the arbiter dismissed a union contention that it was material that the employer treated the payments as wages for federal tax purposes. This was the ruling based on the logic that inflexible categories created by governmental agencies for tax classification should not be employed as determinative criteria in the construction of a collective bargaining agreement.[14]

In a National Distillers Products Corporation case, the arbitrator held that the company was permitted to discontinue a Christmas bonus where some of its contracts contained the "existing benefits" clause and others contained no such clause. The arbitrator held that under those sections, the bonus was not an integral part of the wage structure and therefore it could be discontinued.[15]

At Corland Baking Company, the company reduced the Christmas bonus payments with the employees in a certain year, and it was held that such reduction was permitted under an agreement which did not contain a past practice or past benefit provision. That case is easily distinguishable from the Rockwell-Standard case mentioned above which did contain such a contractual provision.[16]

Under a contract providing for the continuance of "benefits existing prior to the effective date of this agreement," arbitrator Joseph M. Klamon ruled that the employer was not required to continue its practice of paying a Christmas bonus to employees. This was so in view of (1) the employer had accompanied the payment of the bonus with a letter in prior years specifically describing the bonus as a gift that was not a part of the employees' regular pay, and furthermore, stated that similar bonuses in the future could not be guaranteed; and (2) during contract negotiations, the parties had specifically agreed that the contract's existing benefits provision did not include the Christmas bonus.[17]

An examination of this type of decision reveals that it depends on the particular fact situation which is involved. Where the facts definitely show that the Christmas payment has become an integral part of the compensation package, and the agreement includes a past practice or benefit clause, arbiters view the circumstances as implying that payment considerations cannot change without bargaining between the parties. Equally significant to arbitrators is whether or not the employer had tied string around its prior payment, clearly announcing and declaring it as a gift conditional upon its economic ability to continue, and thereby retaining the ability to draw it back unilaterally. However, to preserve its ability to do so, management must be able to clearly establish that it maintained its position on the payment as being a gift during collective bargaining discussions on the subject.

RULINGS IN FAVOR OF THE UNION

Organized labor is equally as concerned about past practice and just as sensitive to its many ramifications as are management's representatives. In any given case, either party may be arguing against, or in favor of, some principle of practice and custom. Union representatives are keenly aware of the role that past practice can play in influencing arbitral decisions. Naturally, whenever the opportunity presents itself, they utilize many of the same arguments regarding the weight and effect to be accorded a practice as does management on other occasions. The union's concern over, and interest in, the impact of practices and customs does not wait to commence at the arbitration hearing table. Early in the union steward's career, he is advised by the parent union organization of the role that past practice can play in certain cases. As part of the overall education and informational program supplied to him by his union affiliate, he is also given advice relative to practices and customs.

Typical of the guidance and advice supplied by the international unions to their local union representatives is the AFL-CIO *Manual for Shop Stewards*. In this booklet, more particularly located within the chapter entitled "What Is a Grievance?" appears a paragraph dealing with this subject titled "Violation of a Past Practice."

A past practice can be the basis for a grievance, particularly in areas where the contract is silent or unclear. However, grievances in this area can be quite complicated and are governed by some of the following rules: 1) A practice, in order to be considered valid, must be repeated over an extended time period. 2) A practice must be accepted explicitly or implicitly by both parties. In the first case, the union and management have formally agreed to the procedure either orally or in writing. Implicit acceptance exists if neither party formally objected to the procedure over a period of time. 3) If a practice violates the contract, either side can demand that the agreement be enforced. 4) If a practice is bad or unsafe, an arbitrator may throw it out on the grounds that it should never have been established in the first place. 5) Past practice grievances arise out of problems such as subcontracting, job descriptions, and work practices like "wash-up time." Because the area of past practices is complex and since a grievance in this area may have implications for an entire plant or company, the international union representative or business agent should be consulted on such matters.

Once in office, and presuming the individual is functioning as a steward in a fairly dynamic labor-management relationship, he soon discovers the materiality of past practice to any claims which he raises on behalf of his constituents. To most management representatives, a grievance, to be considered a validly constituted instrument, must allege a violation of a specific provision as written and expressed in the labor agreement. To many union representatives, a grievance may consist of any management action or inaction about which a worker complains, whether or not the matter complained about is covered by some contractual provision. Although both parties make frequent use of past practice in support of certain positions they take, the scales between the parties in this regard are by no means balanced. The union, more often than management, utilizes the force and effect of past practice in support of claims it makes in the grievance procedure. Since the union is the party which more often makes use of practices and customs in support of its positions, this is probably the circumstance which gives rise to the erroneous belief of many management members that the union is always its sole beneficiary. This is a misconception. As this author believes has already amply been shown, both parties use the argument of past practice in support of, or defense of, positions they take and both parties enjoy the benefits of past practice decisions before arbitrators. It merely seems otherwise because the union is the party which initially files the grievances involving such claims.

We have just discussed cases which supply evidence of this conclusion, where arbitral rulings were rendered in favor of the employer in the resolution of some dispute involving a benefit under the agreement.

Now we shall examine a few where the decision went to the other party, the union.

Under a new agreement which made no mention of a funeral leave allowance, but provided that "all general working conditions shall be maintained at not less than the highest minimum standard in effect at the time of the signing of the agreement," an employer was required by arbitrator Vernon L. Stouffer to continue its prior practice of allowing employees a maximum of three days' funeral leave with pay upon the death of a member of his immediate family. In this case, it had been a regular and consistent policy of the company to grant funeral leave, in addition to paid sick leave. When it changed this practice and began to charge such leave against sick leave, it was operating in contravention to a policy which had ripened into an established practice.[18]

Anaconda Aluminum Company unilaterally discontinued the employee wash-up period and provoked a grievance from the Aluminum Workers International Union. Arbitrator Clair V. Duff decided that the company was without right to do so since (1) by requiring employees to wear work uniforms, it made the changing of clothes on the company's premises an integral part of the employees' principal activity under the Fair Labor Standards Act; (2) the evidence was conclusive that a clearly established past practice existed whereby employees were permitted to leave their work stations about 15 minutes before the end of the shift to wash up, change from work clothes to street clothes, and thus be prepared to punch out at the scheduled time. However, because employees spent five minutes of such time customarily waiting in line to punch out, the employer was required to provide only a 10-minute, rather than a 15-minute wash-up period at the end of each shift.[19]

For over 25 years, another employer had maintained a practice of supplying free coffee to employees during relief and rest periods. This particular agreement stated that "present practices on rest periods shall be continued," and that relief periods would be granted "according to the present practice." Arbitrator Israel Ben Scheiber did not consider this practice negated by the fact that the union had successfully tried to obtain a contractual provision that "benefits now enjoyed, not altered by the agreement, shall remain in effect." It was clear that the free coffee had constituted a plain, definite part of the rest and relief period practices. It had therefore become imbedded in the agreement by the long-continued, well-understood, and mutually concurred in conduct of the parties. Certainly, where the practice had been established for such a long period of time, for at least a quarter of a century, the employees had been given reasonable grounds for believing it would continue. This kind of practice became a part of the contract unless the agreement clearly specified to the contrary. In view of the fact the employer had unilaterally discontinued the practice for almost four months, arbitrator Scheiber directed the company to reestablish the practice and make a payment to the union of $1,500 for distribution to the employees.[20] It is easily imagined that this money award had as its ultimate result the cause of consternation among the union officials. Determining how many cups of coffee were consumed by an average employee on an average day to thus establish his individual monetary reward must have been an interesting chore for this local union.

The Sheridan Machine Company permitted its employees to have coffeepots, cups and hot plates on the premises to make coffee at their place of work. When this practice appeared to be getting out of hand, causing serious interferences with plant efficiencies, the employer decided to put an end to the practice, but to do so by providing the employees with a reasonable substitute. Therefore, they installed in the plant a brewed coffee machine and another coffee vending machine to replace their personal coffee-making equipment which had been ordered removed from the premises. The employer advised the employees of this change by a bulletin board notice which further informed the workers that the proceeds from the machines would go into the employee fund as did that from other vending machines. In the view of arbitrator William Gomberg, their substitute of automatic coffee machines for the employee-operated variety did not constitute an acceptable exchange. Persuasive in his judgment was the fact that it did not use the opportunity of contract negotiations for raising this question. The significance of this principle used by arbiter Gomberg might probably be considered of dubious distinction and materiality to this case. After all, the end result of this long-standing practice of allowing employees to make their own coffee was the product, the coffee itself. The benefit enjoyed by the employees, resulting from the practice of making their own coffee, was the consuming of coffee on company time and premises. Both the union and management agreed that the right to drink coffee during working hours was not an issue — management freely granted this right. Under most circumstances, management would be considered as having supplied a reasonable substitute and alternative which did not interfere with the continuance of the employees' benefit resulting from past practice.[21]

At the Formica Corporation, several departments of the plant had enjoyed two rest periods before lunch and two after lunch. Even though such rest periods were not mentioned in the labor agreement, such had been the case for over five years. When management finally concluded that these rest breaks, as informally followed in the past, were being abused by employees who took more time from work than was needed for personal reasons, it unilaterally acted to formalize more specific regulations. In supporting the union's contentions, the arbiter's remarks relevant to past practice are worthy of examination.

> The amount of off time which an employee is allowed during his shift is clearly a matter comprehended within the broad phrase working conditions. A working condition of this kind may be established without specific written agreement, but as a matter of practice. If such practice has its source in mutual acquiescence of acceptance of both parties, even though such acquiescence may be tacit and may arise by inference from the circumstances. If such practice is uniformly applied, consistently followed, and remains in existence for a sufficient time, it rises to the status of an obligation binding upon both parties and subject to material change only by mutual consent. It is not essential that the practice be uniform throughout the entire plant and affect all the employees in the plant. It may arise in and apply to a particular department, or the practice may differ in different departments depending upon circumstances and conditions which exist in those departments.
>
> The company argues that since the Agreement contains no express provision for continuing in effect established past practices, the general provisions of the management clause permit management to adopt regulations covering rest periods even though they substantially change the practice which has governed these matters for many years. I am unable to agree with that argument. Collective bargaining agreements are negotiated and adopted in a setting of the prior relations of the parties, including past customs and practices. Unless a practice of the kind with which we are here concerned is changed or eliminated by some specific provision of the Agreement or unless the Agreement expressly and clearly revokes all prior practices, the practice remains in effect.[22]

The form that benefits take, arising from some prior practices between parties to a collective bargaining agreement, seems to be of an endless variety.

In a period preceding a first collective bargaining agreement and for five months after its execution, another employer had continued a $50 monthly housing allowance to employees. When the employer unilaterally withdrew its housing allowance payment, it justified its action on its rejection of a general past practice clause as proposed by the union during negotiations. The arbiter did not agree that the employer had the right to make unilateral changes in specific or implied terms of the contract and considered the action unreasonable since it substantially changed the terms and conditions of employment.[23]

The continuance of a long-standing practice of furnishing free milk was sought by the UAW in its grievance with the Ryan Aeronautical Company before aritrator Michael I. Komaroff. For a period of over 10 years, the company had furnished certain employees with free milk, a condition not covered by any contract provision. The company had started this voluntary practice in the belief that it would relieve an unhealthful work condition to which they were exposed on their jobs. Arbiter Komaroff concluded that this long practice made the milk a condition of employment so as to preclude the employer from discontinuing it without first negotiating it with the union. When it unilaterally acted to discontinue the practice, it was operating in violation of this commitment. However, due to the fact that the company did subsequently meet with the union and exchange proposals regarding the matter, and thus met its bargaining obligation, and since this occurred before the arbitration hearing, the arbitrator did not require the company to restore the practice. This was his holding despite the fact the parties had reached an impasse on this matter in their discussions. But, he did require the company to pay each employee a sum of money equivalent to the cost of one pint of milk for each day worked by the eligible employees for the period of time commencing with its unilateral discontinuance of the practice until the date when it finally met and bargained with the union.[24]

The International Brotherhood of Electrical Workers prevented Darling and Company from discontinuing a paid lunch period that had been unilaterally established by the company several years earlier. Arbitrator Joseph M. Klamon ruled that the paid lunch period was so important and so clearly involved with money received by employees for time worked, and so well supported by past practice, that it might not be changed except in direct negotiations with the union.[25]

With Elberta Crate and Box Company, the arbitrator found that the practice of paid lunch periods had come about as a result of an understanding between the parties growing out of a mutual problem and that the employees had been given reasonable grounds for believing it would continue.[26]

Professor Martin Wagner found that a practice at Dayton Steel Foundry Company had existed for 10 or 11 years when the company made a ruling which abolished it. Although this contract granted an employee the right to a 15-minute lunch period, in practice, employees were allowed additional time over and beyond the 15 minutes to leave the department to purchase their lunches. Professor Wagner found the company-established rule to violate the long-established practice and held that the rule was therefore invalid.[27]

Another employer, having undertaken for 18 months to furnish and clean work gloves without cost to its employees, could not unilaterally change this practice and require the employees to share the cost of purchasing and cleaning gloves. Although no express provision of the labor agreement required the furnishing of gloves, arbitrator Marlin A. Volz concluded that the past practice had become binding since (1) the parties had mutually acquiesced in its practice, even though it was not initiated by mutual agreement; (2) the practice was a benefit of value to the employees; and (3) it could not be considered a gratuity since the company appeared to also enjoy a value in return by protecting the employees' safety.[28]

Arbitrator Jules J. Justin, permanent umpire under the agreement between Felsway Shoe Corp., and the Distributive, Processing and Office Workers Union, found the shoe company in violation of its labor agreement by discontinuing a payment of a year-end bonus to employees. This particular labor agreement contained a clause prohibiting reductions in wages and "other fixed financial arrangements." The bonuses had been paid to employees for over 10 years and, therefore, constituted a "fixed financial arrangement" which the employer could not discontinue unilaterally.[29]

Arbitrators have been known to have their decisions overturned in a court of law when a complaining party can establish to the court's satisfaction that the arbiter overstretched his authority allowed under the agreement. Perhaps this possibility occurs by the force of some past practice. This was the final result growing out of a dispute between the Torrington Company and the UAW. An arbiter had held that employees were entitled to receive one hour paid voting time on a general election day in November, even though the contract contained no provision regarding paid voting time. The arbitral ruling turned on the factors that (1) the benefit had been made available to employees for 20 years; (2) the management's rights article did not give the employer the right to unilaterally discontinue the benefit; and (3) the evidence at the hearing did not support the employer's contention that the parties had agreed to discontinue the benefit during negotiations for their current agreement.[30]

Not satisfied with the decision, the employer appealed the matter to the U.S. District Court of Connecticut. Here, the court ruled that the arbitrator had exceeded his authority and thus rendered his award invalid. As mentioned before, the arbiter had based his conclusions on the premise that the practice had become an implied part of the agreement since the contract did not specify that the parties had agreed to discontinue the practice. On this point, the court opined that generally, labor agreements affirmatively state the terms to which the parties agree, not what practices they agree to discontinue. For this reason, and based on a finding that the contract contained no provision regarding paid voting time, and because the employer throughout negotiations had persistently reiterated its position not to grant such benefit, the court vacated the arbitral award.[31]

Gratuities in Arbitration

The term gratuities as it is used here is intended to embrace all of those matters which are not compelled by the terms of the labor agreement, but are initiated by the employer voluntarily, and, typically, unilaterally. Common examples are Christmas turkeys, annual bonuses, picnics, parties, discounts on employee purchases of products, gasoline, and the like.

RULINGS IN FAVOR OF THE EMPLOYER

Telemetal Products, Inc., successfully frustrated an attempt by the IUE under its labor agreement to maintain the payment to employees of a Christmas bonus that had been issued over a prior six-year period. The company stressed that the bonus was a voluntary payment made out of its profits, when, and if earned. When for the first time in its corporate existence, it sustained an operating loss, it did not distribute the bonus. Ruling in favor of the employer, arbitrator Morton Singer made his decision on the following grounds.

> I am convinced that if a bonus is purely a voluntary act, predicated solely on earnings, then no matter how long such bonuses were granted, if the bonus is a voluntary act, it can be stopped, granted, increased or diminished, dependent upon the employer's balance sheet. This fact is supported by the employer's statement that it had experienced a poor year and was in no position to grant a gift at year's end.
> There are certain practices which must be maintained after an agreement is entered into, but such practices are absolute, with no conditions attached....[32]

A reading of the many published cases in which past practice plays a role could readily lead an individual to the conclusion that the most frequently recurring issue is that dealing with an employer's discontinuance of Christmas bonuses and gifts.

Under another contract providing for the continuance of "benefits existing prior to the effective date of this agreement," arbitrator Joseph M. Klamon held that the American Lava Corporation was not required to continue its practice of paying a Christmas bonus to employees. Again, the arbiter's conclusions were significantly influenced by the fact that the company had issued a letter accompanying its bonus payments in prior years specifically describing them as a gift that was not a part of the employees' regular pay, further stating that similar bonuses in the future could not be guaranteed. Also pertinent to the award was the employer's evidence that union negotiators had agreed that the contract's "existing benefits" provision did not include the Christmas bonus. Despite this holding, the arbiter did stop the employer from denying that it had the obligation to pay the bonus in the first Christmas following execution of the contract. This resulted from an expression by the company's negotiators during bargaining that the employer had "hope" that it would be able to pay the bonus that year. Such comments led the employees to have a reasonable expectation of such payment. Therefore, the employer's December 14 announcement of no bonus payment was not supplied to employees in a reasonable time in advance.[33]

A reading of some of these cases could lead to the belief that the employer's financial ability to continue a Christmas bonus payment is an essential part of an arbitrator's consideration. Such an assumption might lead to the wrong conclusion that if a company were in a solid position, its case would fail.

Although it is often a pertinent factor which may influence an arbiter's conclusion favorable to the employer, it is not an essential ingredient. For example, in a case between the South Penn Oil Company and the Oil, Chemical and Atomic Workers International Union, the employer's counsel took the position that financial ability was not relevant to the dispute. Therefore, in arbitrator Clair V. Duff's opinion, he assumed the company had the ability to pay the bonus. Despite the ability of the employer to continue the bonus payment, arbiter Duff ruled that the company had the right to reduce the amount of its annual Christmas bonus since it was not a part of the total contractual wage bargain, but was a gift, given and accepted by the union as a noncontractual benefit. This was his holding in spite of the fact that such bonus had been paid for more than 20 years and in substantially the same amount for several years past.[34]

Arbitrator Emanuel Stein did not think that another agreement "should be so interpreted as to compel the company to convert a friendly and considerate gesture into a binding obligation." An interesting aspect of this case was that it had long been the custom of the company to hold a party for its employees as a part of Christmas observance. However, following an unfortunate incident after one such party, the company unilaterally stopped holding such Christmas parties. Instead, the company gave the employees their individual choice of a turkey or a ham. This it continued to do for two more years. Then, the employer decided for economic reasons not to distribute the turkeys and hams. The arbiter concluded that if there was a "benefit" which the company was bound under the agreement to continue, it was the Christmas party. Yet, the testimony at the hearing clearly disclosed that the company's unilateral discontinuance of these affairs was not challenged by the union, but was instead conceded emphatically by the union. In arbiter Stein's opinion, both the Christmas party and the hams and turkeys constituted the kind of small gift or gratuity appropriate to the season of the year, often given by employers to employees without the connotation of a contractual arrangement.[35]

Considering employees' or a union's attitude toward such matters as these, in an objective way, one would have to concede that it is understandable how they come to consider such gifts or bonuses as a part of their return for services rendered rather than a voluntary gesture of generosity. Nevertheless, the same objective appraisal of such gifts or bonuses can also lead to another understandable conclusion (that is, the universal custom of giving gifts during the Christmas season). It, therefore, would be conceded that usually such gifts are prompted by a spirit of good fellowship, generosity and friendship which is particularly prevalent during such a holiday season. These gifts, when considered in the light of the typically true spirit which generates them, are not conditioned or dependent upon what the receiver has done for the giver. After all, industrial plants are operated by human beings who are not necessarily soulless or as impersonal as often depicted. Their motivations may be quite honorable with a genuine interest in, and concern for, the human welfare of the employee. It is entirely possible, and in fact it might even be deemed probable, that such honorable motivations are the sole driving forces which may move the employer to make the distribution of what would be considered, in any other but the industrial setting, as a gift and not a payment or a contractual obligation.

Travel allowances were another item which a union sought to continue to receive. However, because this contract was silent with regard to travel allowances and was without any provision requiring the continuance of existing benefits, the arbitrator deciding the dispute held that it was merely a gratuity which the employer was at liberty to discontinue.[36]

In a recent decision, arbitrator Edwin R. Teple expressed this opinion: "From a review of the cases involving such things as Thanksgiving turkeys, Christmas hams, and Christmas bonuses, the trend of arbitral opinion appears to be in support of the employer's position that these are gratuitous activities." This remark was expressed when he upheld the employer's position at the Falstaff Brewing Company. Going back several years, in 1956, the Fellowship Club at the plant of this employer sponsored a summer picnic for employees and their families. Again in 1957, this organization, which had no connection with a union, held another family picnic. Then, in 1958, this club became defunct — but, the employer sponsored the same affair and invited the entire plant. It continued to sponsor the outing for the next 10 years with attendance and costs rising from 263 people for $857 in 1958, to 928 people for $2,423 in 1967. However, compelled by economy considerations, the employer posted a notice to employees in August 1968 that its family picnic would have to be discontinued. One of the unions representing the employees instantly grieved and urged that the picnic had ripened into a fixed obligation, and although the agreement was silent with respect to it, the picnic constituted a benefit under the contractual arrangement. The employer argued that the affair had been unilaterally established and controlled and as a gratuity was subject to unilateral abandonment. Arbiter Teple agreed with the company that the picnic had been offered as a gesture of goodwill and the affair rested within the control of its volunary sponsor.[37]

To sum up, it is perhaps advisable to refer to the opinion of one arbitrator who took the pains in a 1960 decision to set forth eight criteria for distinguishing between binding past practices and gratuities. The arbitrator to be thanked for this contribution was Burton B. Turkus, and any credit which flows from the benefit of the following listing should be attibuted to him.

His introductory remarks are also worthy of review:

> The problem here presented is one which has vexed arbitrators with considerable frequency in the past. Certain indexes are sought with such regularity in these cases as to be signposts for future travellers down this, at times, tortuous road. Some of these are:
> 1. Does the practice concern a major condition of employment
> 2. Was it established unilaterally
> 3. Was it administered unilaterally
> 4. Did either of the parties seek to incorporate it into the body of the written agreement
> 5. What is the frequency of repetition of the "practice"
> 6. Is the "practice" a long-standing one
> 7. Is it specific and detailed
> 8. Do the employees rely on it[38]

As may be concluded, arbiter Turkus was motivated to make these remarks while wrestling with a case involving the weight and effect to be accorded to a past practice. He further remarked that seldom do such cases produce replies to these questions which are always negative. The determinative force comes from the judgment as to which of these, and how many, are answered with sufficient cumulative force and frequency as to sustain the position of one party or the other.

RULINGS IN FAVOR OF THE UNION

Needless to say, some arbitration decisions involving Christmas bonuses and other alleged types of gratuities do occasionally go to the union. It will be interesting to apply the criteria cited above as contributed by Turkus to the case situations which will now be examined. It will become readily apparent where management failed to measure up to the crucial tests.

Arbitrator Donald A. Crawford, a highly respected member of the National Academy of Arbitrators before his untimely death, decided a dispute between the Pennsylvania Forge Company and the International Association of Machinists. Here the employer had paid a Christmas bonus to employees in a fixed amount for a period of 19 successive years, even though the contract was silent on the subject. Also, this particular agreement did not contain a clause continuing existing benefits. Mr. Crawford ruled against the employer, holding that it did not have the right to discontinue such bonus since it had been considered and discussed in connection with the parties' contract negotiations. Prior to final execution of the agreement, the employer had stated that it "assumed" the union's strike would have no effect on the bonus. This certainly implied a commitment that the bonus would be continued. Still another consideration in this grievance was that the bonus was incorporated as part of the wage settlement under the contract to preserve the amount of average negotiated wage increase. The arbiter dismissed the employer's argument that it could not afford to make the payment. This was so since it was found that the employees were entitled to the bonus under the contract, and that the company had never connected the bonus to its profit situation but had made the bonus payment in poor as well as in good years.[39]

Under another contract, for approximately 20 years, the company had distributed cash gifts to employees each year during the Christmas holiday season. In the most recent years, the amount of such payments had remained fixed. Due to a decline in profits, the company decided that economies were in order and discontinued the bonus; however, it did distribute turkeys or hams to the employees. Significant to the arbitrator in holding for the union was that the agreement required the employer to maintain all previous conditions of employment relating to wages, hours of work, and general working conditions. The employees were not told that the gifts would be based on any particular level of profits or similar fluctuating factors. Over the years, the employees had understandably come to the conclusion that the regular Christmas bonuses were an integral part of the wage structure.[40]

Another employer found itself unable to discontinue a Christmas bonus under its first union contract when an arbitrator ruled that such bonus was not a gratuity or a gift as contended by the company, since, in a circular sent to the employees, the employer had equated the bonus with wages paid, thereby conveying the impression that it was an integral part of the wage structure. Further, the same circular also indicated that the company considered the bonus as a deferred compensation for services rendered, and as a term or condition of employment. It had made this payment to its employees every year in the five years preceding the coming of the union. Despite the fact the parties had not discussed the bonus during their initial negotiations and that the contract was silent on the subject, and contained no "maintenance of past practice and privilege clause," the principle that the contract may subsume the continuation of existing conditions was applicable.[41] Plainly, in this situation the employer had, by its own admission, related the bonus payment to services rendered and wages paid. There was no attempt to call it a gift or a gratuity, or to make its continuation dependent upon economic factors. Once having committed itself in writing in the circulars distributed to employees, it became incumbent upon the employer to discuss the matter with the union during negotiations and "bargain it out" if it did not wish to maintain the payment.

According to two authorities,

> A collective bargaining agreement should be deemed, unless a contrary intention is manifest, to carry forward for its term the major terms and conditions of employment, not covered by the agreement, which prevailed when the agreement was executed ... thus, if a union were to protest a company's unilateral discontinuance of a hospitalization plan which the company had voluntarily maintained for a considerable period, an arbitrator ... should sustain the union's grievance even though the plan was not mentioned in the collective bargaining agreement.[42]

4. Past Practice Versus Management Rights

Ordinarily, the labor contract has among its provisions a statement relative to the employer's management of its plant and the direction of the working force. The following passage contains language typical of such a contractual statement in which the employer has endeavored to identify comprehensively its several prerogatives.

Rights of Management

Except as otherwise specifically provided in this Agreement, the Employer has the sole and exclusive right to exercise all the rights or functions of management, and the exercise of any such rights or functions shall not be subject to the grievance or arbitration provisions of this Agreement.

Without limiting the generality of the foregoing, as used herein, the term "Rights of Management" includes:

(a) the right to manage the plant;
(b) the right to schedule working hours;
(c) the right to establish, modify or change work schedules or standards;
(d) the right to direct the working forces, including the right to hire, promote, or transfer any employee;
(e) the location of the business, including the establishment of new plants or departments, divisions or subdivisions thereof, and the relocation or closing of plants, departments, divisions or subdivisions thereof;
(f) the determination of products to be manufactured or sold or services to be rendered or supplied;
(g) the determination of the layout and the machinery, equipment or materials to be used in the business;
(h) the determination of processes, techniques, methods, and means of manufacture, maintenance or distribution, including any changes or adjustments of any machinery or equipment;
(i) the determination of the size and character of inventories;
(j) the determination of financial policy, including accounting procedures, prices of goods or services rendered or supplied, and customer relations;
(k) the determination of the organization of each production, service maintenance or distribution department, division or subdivision or

69

any other production maintenance, service or distribution unit deemed appropriate by the Employer;

(l) the selection, promotion, or transfer of employees to supervisory or managerial positions or to positions outside of the bargaining unit;

(m) the determination of the size of the working force;

(n) the allocation and assignment of work to employees;

(o) the determination of policy affecting the selection or training of new employees;

(p) the establishment of quality and quantity standards and the judgment of the quality and quantity of workmanship required;

(q) the control and use of the plant property, material, machinery, or equipment;

(r) the scheduling of operations and the determination of the number and duration of shifts;

(s) the determination of safety, health, and property protection measures for the plant;

(t) the establishment, modification and enforcement of plant rules or regulations, which are not in direct conflict with any of the provisions of this Agreement;

(u) the transfer of work from one job to another or from one plant, department, division or other plant unit to another;

(v) introduction of new, improved or different production, maintenance, service or distribution methods or facilities or a change in existing methods or facilities;

(w) the placing of production, service, maintenance or distribution work with outside contractors or subcontractors;

(x) the determination of the amount of supervision necessary;

(y) the right to terminate, merge or sell the business or any part thereof;

(z) the transfer of employees from one job to another or from one plant, department, division or other plant unit to another.

It is agreed that the enumeration of management prerogatives above shall not be deemed to exclude other management prerogatives not specifically enumerated above.[1]

The above is representative of an attempt by an employer to detail, as comprehensively as possible, those rights, functions and prerogatives it wishes to ensure will be understood as retained by it. The majority of labor agreements contain a statement of management's rights (rather than have the matter unmentioned), although the majority are not as detailed and comprehensive in their phrasing as the above provision.

Whether or not the labor agreement contains a management prerogative clause or a management reservation of rights clause, it is a well-established principle in labor-management relations that all the powers and authorities not bargained away are reserved by the employer. The absence of such a clause does not signify that the company has surrendered or waived any powers or prerogatives other than those waived or surrendered in its contractual relations with the union. Such a circumstance remains despite a contract being silent about this subject.

It is also a fairly well-settled proposition that an employer has a perpetual right in the enforcement of its rights and privileges, so long as it is not done for a discriminatory or malicious purpose. For this reason, management's failure to enforce all of its rights will ordinarily not constitute a waiver of such rights in the eyes of most arbitrators, except where the circumstances mislead the union to its prejudice or injury, or where there are elements of estoppel present. The theory of estoppel is best described as the effect of the voluntary conduct of a party whereby it is precluded from asserting rights which it perhaps might have otherwise achieved by contract, as against another party who has in good faith relied upon such conduct and has been led thereby to change its position, and who on its part acquires some corresponding right either of contract or remedy.

Numerous are the examples of cases where the employer has waived, or not exercised a particular contract right, without such waiver resulting in a binding precedent for all cases of like circumstance in the future. But in an instant case, an employer's failure to exercise its right in prior cases can produce a result damaging to its interests. For example, a discharge grievance was ruled to be arbitrable although the union had not observed the contractual time limits for filing the grievance, where (1) the employer was aware the grievance was pending; and (2) the parties had not observed or insisted upon the observance of strict time limits in accordance with the contract in the past.[2]

This case is an excellent example of the results obtained by an employer who waived a right it might have otherwise exercised under contract, and by doing so gave an arbiter no choice but to estop it from exercising the forfeited right in the instant case. There are a good many published arbitration awards, particularly of this time limit variety, where arbiters have ruled that management waived its opportunity to protest a grievance's procedural defects, because of management's practice of not exercising its contractual right to protest in the past. However, in cases where the union has charged that the employer agreed to waive some contractual right, arbiters have held that such a claim must be proven "by clear, convincing and definite evidence."[3]

Fortunately for management, arbitrators seem to have made a distinction between practices which are binding and those which are not, by giving consideration to whether it involves something of value and benefit to employees, or instead involves the denial or continuance of a basic managerial right essential to management's operation of the business and direction of the work force. There is some hesitation on the part of arbitrators to allow unions to use some unwritten force to effectively diminish some inherent management prerogative. This conclusion will be supported as several relevant cases are examined.

There are some kinds of functions which, absent any limitation thereof in the contract, clearly fall within the area of management's functions. The establishment of reasonable rules governing employee conduct is one such function.

During the term of an agreement, it is commonplace to see a need arise for the promulgation of certain rules and regulations which are in addition to those already established. Ever-changing work situations produce new and different operational problems which often have to be given coverage by new or different work rules. Where rules have been established but do not contain a schedule of the specific punishment to be meted out for particular offenses put into effect by either agreement, company rules or practices, the penalty to be imposed for a given offense rests in the reasonable discretion of the employer. Generally speaking, arbitrators have ruled that they do not have the right to substitute their judgment for that of management except where there has been abuse of such discretion. However, the union organization does not always concede to this principle and often views management's issuance of rules as a threatening action which it must, as a matter of policy, contest through grievance and arbitration. But, the overwhelming majority of arbiters will hold that unless expressly prohibited by some express provision of the contract, management has the right to issue rules and does maintain unilateral determination of such a matter.

On the other hand, there is no dispute that the company's reasonable application and administration of such rules are a valid, contestable subject by the union. However, when the contract protects the employees against discipline or discharge unless for just cause, as agreements commonly do today, the question of what constitutes reasonable and adequate grounds for discipline or discharge is removed from this exclusive area of management discretion. Therefore, it follows that the company's unilaterally determined concepts of the extent of discipline to be imposed in a given case are certainly subject to challenge by employees and the union. Again, the role of past practice can be a significant factor in the final outcome of such grievance disputes.

A typical example of this occurred between the Metal Specialty Company and the International Association of Machinists in a controversy decided by arbitrator Marlin M. Volz. This labor agreement reserved to the company the right to "require employees to observe company rules and regulations not inconsistent with the provisions of this agreement." Proceeding with the assumption that its new rule was not inconsistent with the contract, the employer promulgated a plant rule limiting employees' use of vending machines to the 10-minute breaks in the middle of the first and second halves of their work shift. Although the practice antedating the installation of the vending machines had been for employees to break every hour, this practice had constituted an abuse which had contributed substantially to a drop in production. Here, the agreement was silent on the question of work breaks or the use of vending machines, and thus left the matter open for determination by practice or the adoption of reasonable plant rules. Holding for the employer, the arbiter did regulate the situation by requiring that the rules should be applied to accord with the past practice by allowing employees a four-minute nonvending-machine break each hour.[4]

A similar case occurred between the Magnavox Company and the Allied Industrial Workers. The arbitrator for this dispute was John Day Larkin. His ruling was that this employer had the right to promulgate and enforce a new plant rule forbidding employees the use of food and beverage vending machines in the plant at times other than lunch and rest periods. Despite the past practice of unrestricted use of such machines for 18 years, the employer had not agreed in writing to permit employees free and unrestricted use of such machines. Moreover, the labor agreement reserved to the employer the right to publish new rules and further provided that absence from work, except for personal need and rest periods, "shall be by permission." Interesting in this decision was the arbitrator's dismissal of the union's argument that the rule was discriminatory in that it was not applied to salaried employees. He disregarded this union contention on the premise that the language of the agreement pertained only to those within the unit and in no way affected the company dealings with the personnel of excluded groups.[5]

The question of the effect of past practice became secondary in importance in the light of the language of a management prerogative in another agreement which reads as follows:

> Except as expressly limited by the terms of this agreement, the company retains the sole and exclusive right to operate its plant and direct its working force, and take any action affecting any or all of its employees without consultation with the union.

In the opinion of the arbitrator, the last excerpt quoted above was too sweeping to warrant a conclusion that it was merely a more explicit expression of the inherent rights of management. By this language in the contract, it appeared to the arbiter that the union had conceded to management the right to make unilaterally a change from fixed to rotating shifts in a certain department. Equally as persuasive to his conclusions was the fact that the agreement was silent with regard to specifically forbidding such a change to rotating shifts. For these reasons, arbitrator Paul Prasow was of the opinion that a determination of whether past practice favored the union seemed to have little bearing on the outcome of the dispute.[6]

A change in the hours of the work day by management was upheld by arbitrator B. Meredith Reid. The established work day had run from 8 A.M. to 5 P.M. and was in effect at the time the contract was adopted and was a part of the company's rules. The union contended that for these reasons it had become an implied part of the contract and could not be changed without the union's consent. Arbiter Reid did not agree with this argument. In the absence of a contractual provision to the contrary, the employer had the right to unilaterally change to a 7 A.M. to 4 P.M. work day. Because the prior established hours had been incorporated in a company rule in effect when the contract was executed, such rule did not freeze into that agreement the hours of starting and stopping work. This was so for the reason given earlier, namely, the changing of company rules was a prerogative of management. In the absence of arbitrary, capricious or other discriminatory abuse, such company-established rules could not be set aside solely because there were unilateral changes made.[7]

The Globe-Union Company had a long-standing practice of assigning to timekeepers the work of filling out employees' time records. In the absence of a contractual provision to the contrary, arbitrator Clarence M. Updegraff ruled that the employer had the right to institute a new policy requiring employees to fill out their own time records. Employees who refused to do so on the grounds that the company lacked the right to discontinue the long practice of assigning timekeepers to do such work were considered by the arbiter as properly subject to discipline. Although there was no question as to the company's right to institute a new practice of requiring employees to fill out their own time cards showing the work performed and the applicable rate, the arbiter did feel that the employer was obliged to restudy the jobs to determine whether such work took more of the employees' time than was formerly required of them in keeping certain other records. If so, it was required to make an allowance in the rates for such extra time.[8]

Under another agreement which reserved to the company the right to direct its work force, arbitrator Livingston Smith allowed the employer to institute a rotation plan in which certain employees were required to shift from one operating unit to another at regular intervals in order to familiarize them with operations of both units. The union contended that the prior practice of assigning employees to fixed stations represented a benefit and fell within the meaning of a contractual provision requiring the continuance of all existing benefits for the life of the contract. This argument the arbitrator rejected.[9]

The International Chemical Workers union agreed that under its contract with the U.S. Rubber Company it had always been a practice to fill in for absenteeism by holding over or calling out a qualified technician. On vacation replacement, it was scheduled overtime. Although this contract provided that "in case of absenteeism, including vacations, the absent employees will be replaced with the employee having the lowest overtime at the time the absence occurs," such provision did not obligate the employer to fill temporary vacancies. In the view of arbitrator Paul M. Hebert, it merely provided the manner in which vacancies must be filled if they are filled at all. The language did not indicate a clear intention to modify the reserved right of the company to determine the size of its work force. The company's past practice of filling vacancies created by vacations and other temporary absences of employees did not create a continuing obligation to fill such temporary vacancies during periods of reduced production.[10]

Arbitrator Sylvester Garrett was called upon to determine the effect of past practice on the right of the employer to institute a new method of testing applicants for promotion to craft jobs. The Steelworkers union in this dispute claimed that the employer's prior means of testing applicants constituted an established practice so as to require its continuation. However, the evidence demonstrated that there was no clearly uniform procedure in testing applicants previously, and in addition, the union was unable to show that the new method materially prejudiced employees' rights to obtain promotions. This occurred under an agreement which gave the company the right to make initial determinations regarding employees' qualifications for promotions to craft jobs, but at the same time, required the continuation of all established practices.

Although the new questionnaire utilized by the company was of a more formal and comprehensive nature, and even perhaps of a more formidable character, it served the same purpose as did the earlier testing. Also, the test results were not conclusive but were furnished to supervisors who then made final selections to fill positions in journeymen classifications. There was also no limitation on the number of times an employee could return and take the test over again. The arbiter also believed that the new method of testing provided certain benefits to employees that were lacking in the former testing, namely, that it greatly reduced the possibility of error and the element of favoritism. Also, if an employee did not concur with the test results, he could protest management's decision through the grievance and arbitration procedures.[11]

In exercising its right to direct its work force according to its best judgment, the National Container Corporation reduced the size of the work crews on printing presses and eliminated the requirement of 100 percent inspection of work by crews. The Pulp and Sulphite Workers Union protested this management action and the matter ended up before arbitrator A.R. Marshall. In view of the fact that (1) nothing in the agreement limited the company's right to change the methods of production in the interests of efficiency; and (2) the reduction in crew size did not make the work load of the remaining employees too easy; and (3) the earnings opportunities under this new method of operation were set on the basis of fair and accurate time studies; and (4) the actual earnings of employees on the reduced crews were primarily the same as when larger crews were operating, the arbiter ruled that the employer had not violated the contract. Rejected was the union's contention that the employer had disturbed work practices and that such changes could only result through negotiations.[12]

The Steelworkers union challenged the right of the Carrier Corporation to unilaterally install time clocks for the purpose of recording hours worked and other payroll data. Employees manually filled out the time cards previously. Arbitrator Harry J. Dworkin considered management's action a legitimate and proper exercise of its prerogative under a broad management's rights clause. The agreement contained no reference to time clocks and the change did not impose any appreciable burden upon employees as compared with the prior practice. Therefore, it could not be construed as a change in a working condition or an established past practice that had to first be negotiated with the union.[13]

A clause in the contract of the Hotpoint Company specified that established practices affecting employees not specifically covered by the contract "shall not be changed or eliminated prior to discussion with the union." The UAW contended the employer violated the agreement when it failed to call a member of the production control group in for inventory work. On prior occasions, it had been company practice to use production control employees for inventory work. However, this unit had already been discontinued at the time the inventory had been taken and the employees from that group had been reassigned to considerably changed duties. Upholding the employer's action, arbitrator Clarence M. Updegraff concluded that if the company had the authority to discontinue the production control unit and the usual job duties of the employees, it naturally followed that it would also have commensurate authority to change its practice with respect to using them on inventory work. Relevant to the decision was the fact that the inventory work was an infrequent, minor and incidental aspect of these employees' tasks.[14]

A rather unique contractual provision at the Corning Packaging Company provided that existing benefits "may be changed by the company in whole or in part, or completely withdrawn when in its judgment such action becomes necessary after notice to and consultation with the union." This same labor agreement contained another clause which stated that no change in existing working conditions "will be made except for the purpose of improving the production or the efficiency of the plant." So, despite a 14-year practice of granting 20-minute paid lunch periods, arbitrator Jacob D. Hyman rejected the Glass Worker union's grievance and ruled that the employer had the right, after its notice to and consultation with the union, to institute 30-minute unpaid lunch periods on two-shift operations. The change in the lunch period was a change in the working conditions or a withdrawal of a benefit and therefore within the meaning of the contract.[15]

The above-cited cases will provide a general flavor of arbitral decisions where management's exercise of its managerial discretions and prerogatives has been challenged by the union. An attempt was made to provide the reader with sufficient variety of fact situations and circumstances to supply a broader insight into arbitral rationale. We shall now move along into an examination of a number of specific areas in which the clash between the union's claim of past practice and the employer's exercise of managerial prerogatives has produced the need for arbitral dispute settlements.

Subcontracting

The term subcontracting (contracting out, farming out) pertains to the practice of having certain steps in a manufacturing process, plant maintenance, equipment or machine or property erection or repair, or other work functions, performed by outside contractors, using their own work forces.

More often than not, the management's motivating reasons are economic — in other words, to have the work performed on less expensive terms. However, it may also be done because the prime employer does not have sufficient manpower to accomplish the given task, or does not possess the technical skills, or does not possess certain unique machinery or equipment, or needs the work performed within time limitations it cannot meet with its own work force. Significant to the study here, past practice can be a most relevant factor.

RULINGS IN FAVOR OF THE EMPLOYER

Problems involving subcontracting are always troublesome to both parties under a labor agreement. More often than otherwise, such cases are decided on the basis of the particular fact situations and circumstances of each specific dispute, and the contract language, if any, which governs or regulates such work. However, in certain situations past practice can be a decisive or influencing factor in an arbitrator's findings. A few illustrations where this has been the case follow.

The labor agreement between Convey-All Corporation and the International Union of Electrical, Radio and Machine Workers did not contain a provision expressly barring contracting work out. The employer assigned a millwright outside the bargaining unit to drive his truck with certain tools and equipment to a work site 50 miles away where other millwrights were engaged in a long job. The union protested this assignment, relying upon the recognition and seniority clauses of the contract, and the fact that truck driver was a mutually agreed upon contractual job classification. Significant to arbitrator Samuel S. Kates in ruling for the employer was the fact that at the time the contract was entered, not only had the company's transportation of tools and equipment been done by common carrier truckers and its own truck driver, but also, a long-established practice had existed under which, when a rush job was involved, an independent millwright would drive such tools and equipment in one of the company's trucks. There was no evidence that any bargaining unit member actually lost time as a result of the incident; it did not appear that any diminution of the bargaining unit membership resulted or would likely result from this occurrence; this specific incident was related to an exceptional rather than an ordinary situation; and it was analogous to such special situations in the past.[16]

In the above-cited case, the evidence at the hearing indicated a reasonably uniform and consistent practice by the employer in its subcontracting actions when the fact situations and circumstances were akin to the given case. In this next dispute, the fact that past practice was mixed and not uniform and consistent appeared to influence somewhat the arbitral conclusions.

In the Celotex Corporation, a contract provision stated that all work "customarily performed" by employees shall continue to be performed by employees, "unless in the judgment of the company, such work should be performed by outside contractors," and also stated that the decision as to subcontracting would be based on the availability of a qualified working force. In the past, employees under the labor agreement had occasionally performed work of the type which the company subcontracted, and this provoked the instant grievance. The fact that the employees had performed such work previously did bring the work in question under the restrictions of the contractual provision. However, the contract did enable the employer to retain judgment over the matter and did not require that such work belonged to the employees exclusively in the future. Secondly, the company was able to introduce substantial evidence at the arbitration hearing which indicated that work similar to that involved in the instant case had been done by outside contractors on prior occasions. The evidence of this practice merely demonstrated that the question of whether the work would be done inside or outside would vary depending upon the judgment of the company as allowed by the agreement.[17]

National Airlines, Inc., had an agreement with the Airline Employees Association which embraced employees in the service of the airlines who were employed within the continental United States. For a period of 15 years, the refueling of its aircraft at the Tampa, Florida, location had been performed by the company with its own employees in the ramp agent classification. Despite this long-standing practice, the company entered into a contract with an outside concern for the refueling of its aircraft at that location. The six ramp agents who had been doing this work were transferred to other duties. Since the company's business had been increasing, no layoff resulted. The union promptly grieved.

The following factors were controlling in the decision of arbitrator James C. Vadakin in his ruling in favor of the employer: (1) no specific limitation on subcontracting appeared in the contract; (2) the arbiter did not imply a limitation from the job description of the ramp agent which stated that he "may refuel aircraft"; (3) the history of the bargaining between the parties revealed that the union had made several unsuccessful attempts to obtain subcontracting restrictions in the agreement; (4) despite the above-mentioned practice at Tampa, for several years the employer had subcontracted refueling operations at several other terminals and its right to do so had been upheld in two prior arbitration awards; (5) there was good faith motivation on the part of the company in that its action was stimulated by considerations of economy and efficiency; and (6) no employees were laid off.[18]

Another contract stated that the employer would not contract out work customarily performed by bargaining unit employees. But, the agreement further stated that the employer might continue to subcontract work that it had subcontracted prior to 1962. Arbitrator Sidney L. Cahn heard the employer's undenied evidence that an employee of an outside contractor had been performing porters' duties since 1957. This was so even though the employer still retained other porters in its employ. He was of the opinion that the period of 1957 to 1964 constituted a custom accepted by the parties within the meaning of the contractual provision.[19]

In a dispute between the Singer Company and the IUE in which the union contended that a past practice existed prohibiting certain work, the employer turned the tables on the union at the arbitration hearing by providing undenied evidence which disclosed that for over 20 years the company had subcontracted carpentry-partition work, both new and old. Not only did the union fail to establish the existence of past practice prohibiting the work, but other evidence introduced by the employer also disclosed that as far back as 10 years prior, the union sought to obtain a provision prohibiting subcontracting which was effectively repelled by the employer, with the contract remaining silent on the subject.[20]

Another arbitrator upheld an employer's right to have roof repairs made by a subcontractor where its attempts to effect minor economies impaired no paramount contractual rights of the union. Even though bargaining unit employees had done such work on occasion in the past, it appeared that all of the unit employees worked either a full 40-hour week or some overtime during the period in question. However, although he held for the employer under this contract, which contained no specific restrictions upon subcontracting, because of the existence of the past practice, he did direct the employer, in the future, to negotiate with the union on subcontracting of work which under past practice had been awarded to bargaining unit employees.[21]

One of the elements of past practice which must be present in order to make it an effective argument before an arbitrator is knowledge and acquiescence by the other party. Where this element is present, arbitrators have considered past practice significant. This was true in a dispute at the Collins Radio Company, decided by arbitrator Roy R. Ray, where the employer had a long history of subcontracting. It had subcontracted production work of all kinds for several years, including painting, plumbing, electrical and carpenter work. Also, it had subcontracted all janitorial work in certain areas of its buildings. The union was fully aware of this subcontracting. In contract negotiations, the union was advised that the company would subcontract all janitorial services in certain buildings. For several years, until the instant grievance was filed by the union, it never officially protested the subcontracting of janitor work. In the light of this significant factor, and where the employer had acted in good faith and for reasons of economy and efficiency, and the subcontracting did not present a threat to the scope of the bargaining unit nor represent an attempt on the part of the employer to evade his contractual responsibilities, the arbiter held that no contractual violation resulted.[22]

A similar ruling was rendered by arbitrator Clair V. Duff where an established practice of the Union Carbide Metals Company of subcontracting work was well known to the Oil, Chemical and Atomic Workers Union. Here, the employer subcontracted the work of modernizing furnaces instead of assigning such work to its maintenance employees. The union alleged this constituted a violation of the contract's recognition clause. The agreement was silent, containing no limitation upon subcontracting in the negotiations which took place during the period in which the modernization subcontract was let. Since the employer had made a number of such contracts over a period of ten years or more with the union's knowledge, and since the present dispute did not constitute a change or enlargement of that practice, arbiter Duff sustained the company's action.[23]

It will be readily noted that past practice was not the single controlling factor in the decisions of these cited cases. Standing alone, it would not overcome other compelling factors which might operate singly or in combination to determine the outcome of such a dispute. The other factors referred to which are customarily looked upon by arbitrators as influential in their decisions follow shortly herein. Therefore, to reemphasize, the practices and customs of the parties which surround their subcontracting activities are a factor which is considered by arbitrators and accorded some weight. However, in those cases where the following factors have been substantially satisfied by the company, in the judgment of the arbitrator, past practice can play a persuasive role in influencing the final decision.

The following are the criteria referred to above. The list is not intended to be all-inclusive, but for the most part, it covers the more dominant and influential factors in arbitral awards on subcontracting.

(1) *The history of negotiations between parties.* Has the subject of subcontracting been discussed between the parties during collective bargaining? Has the union submitted demands to the employer which if adopted would have limited or prohibited management's right to subcontract?[24]

(2) *Contract language.* In the light of the bargaining history mentioned above, which contractual provisions, if any, refer to or cover specifically the subject of subcontracting? Is the contract silent despite a union attempt to obtain restrictive language? If the agreement provides certain limitations on management's right to subcontract, are such restrictions as broad and as wide as demanded by the union — or did the union obtain fewer limitations than it sought?

(3) *The effect of management's subcontracting action on the union.* Arbitrators are often interested in the answer to the question of whether the subcontracting action was taken to deliberately injure, undermine or discriminate [against] the union. In other words, was its action prejudicial or discriminatory in any way? Did it materially prejudice the status of the bargaining unit?[25]

(4) *The duration and regularity of the subcontracting action.* Was this a one-time occurrence, an incident that would repeat itself but only spasmodically, or would it be done on a frequent and repeating basis? Whether the subcontracting action represented a temporary condition or one having permanent status can be meaningful to an arbitrator.[26]

(5) *The availability of facilities and equipment.* Did the employer possess sufficient and appropriate facilities, materials and equipment to accomplish the task subcontracted? Was the work performed beyond

his capability in the light of this question? If such was not instantly available, could it have been readily obtained with a relatively small economic investment?[27]

(6) *The effect on the unit.* As a result of the subcontracting action, were any employees laid off, displaced or have their earnings materially reduced? Were employees laid off at the time people who could have been reasonably and readily recalled and who had appropriate skills to perform the work? Did employees experience a reduction in over-time opportunities?[28]

(7) *The availability of qualified employees.* Were employees readily available in sufficient numbers and in possession of skills and ability adequate to perform the required work?[29]

(8) *The type of work.* Was the nature of the subcontracting work such as to require it be done outside for reasons of security or economy? Was it an unusual task or work which constituted an emergency? Were there time limitations on its accomplishment which could only be made by having it performed outside? If it was done to achieve economies, were such economies realized, and if so, how substantial were the savings?[30]

Added to this list, of course, would be past practice. In this connection, arbitrators are always interested in whether the work has been contracted out in the past, and if so, to what extent. They are also concerned with the frequency and the regularity of such practices, and how well known they generally were to the union.

RULINGS IN FAVOR OF THE UNION

The Schmutz Mfg. Co. was held to be in violation of its contract when it permitted three supervisors to spend virtually all of their time in production work. It was true that a past practice existed here which antedated the advent of the union which allowed such supervisors to perform production work. This practice was for naught in the employer's defense of its action in the face of explicit and clear contract language which controlled the performance of bargaining unit work by supervisors.[31] Clearly, in this instance management had given up its right to exercise managerial discretion over this particular area, and therefore, past practice had no impact whatsoever.

Past practice was determinative of a subcontracting issue between the Haddon Craftsmen, Inc., and the International Brotherhood of Bookbinders Union. This agreement contained a provision making any dispute over a change in "job condition or practice" subject to the grievance and arbitration procedures. The contract did not contain any expressed restriction on the assignment of production work to supervisors. In view of the above-mentioned contract language which permitted the union to grieve, the union properly protested the employer's transfer of certain work to supervisors which in the past had always been performed by nonsupervisory employees. The implication of the contract language was that existing conditions and practices were to continue during the contract term unless there was some persuasive reason for changing them. In this instance, the employer provided no persuasive reason for changing the practice in question. It was true that the change did produce some savings in labor costs, but it was for the effect of taking work away from regular production workers and thus operated to their detriment.[32]

Under another agreement between the Tenneco Oil Company and the Oil, Chemical and Atomic Workers International Union, language stated that the employer "will make every reasonable effort to use its available work force and equipment to avoid having its work performed by outside contractors." During this hearing, the company presented its honest and reasonable judgment that it would have been insufficient to allow production workers to work overtime on their regularly scheduled days to do work performed by the subcontractors. This defense did not take into consideration the interests of the employees in the bargaining unit, and the reasonableness of the decision to subcontract could not be forwarded solely from the employer's point of view. Such an argument did not constitute compliance with the contract where the union had (1) capably shown that a past practice existed of performing the disputed work in this very manner; and (2) produced testimony clearly indicating that critical skills were not required for adequate performance of the work.[33]

In another dispute, management's ability to prove a past practice of subcontracting, of which the union had prior notice, did not estop the union from seeking arbitration of the company's unilateral discontinuance of its night shift and the subcontracting of the work. The arbiter here did not bind the union to a pre–collective bargaining past practice prior to the time the union was the bargaining representative. Incidental to this conclusion was the fact that the prebargaining subcontracting did not involve the layoff of bargaining unit employees as had occurred in the instant case. Therefore, under this agreement, which contained no express prohibition against subcontracting, the arbiter ruled that the employer violated the agreement by unilaterally discontinuing the night shift and subcontracting the work to a closely affiliated subsidiary. Of some influence to the arbiter's conclusions was the fact that the subsidiary rehired the primary employer's laid-off employees to perform the work at nonunion wages and under nonunion conditions. The company's action did not meet the tests of reasonableness and good faith. The company argued that continuance of the night-shift operations would produce continuing losses. However, if such was not econom-ically justified, the company also made no apparent effort to increase the day-shift operations to maximum output by recruiting additional man-power from the night shift. Secondly, its subcontracting arrangement failed to provide the basic circumstances in which a truly independent contractor relationship could exist.

Thirdly, it took this action without notice to or negotiations with the union representing the employees. In the view of the arbiter, the simplest worded labor agreement implies good faith and fair dealing. The recognition of the union as the exclusive representative of the employees carried with it an obligation to refrain from arbitrarily or unreasonably reducing the scope of the bargaining representative.[34]

Arbitrator Samuel S. Kates found implied restrictions in the labor agreement and held that the Eaton Manufacturing Company violated contract provisions relating to recognition of the union and seniority when it retained an employee of an outside contractor in full-time work during a time when five bargaining unit employees had been laid off. The employer's showing of a past practice that the work had been performed full time for some period, and that knowledge of this was chargeable to the union, did not indicate the union's acquiescence to the practice in the view of this arbiter, since it appeared that for most of this period there were no unit employees on layoff.[35]

Job Assignments

RULINGS IN FAVOR OF THE EMPLOYER

A job assignment dispute arose between the Waterfront Employer's Association of the Pacific Coast and the Longshoremen's Union in the Portland area. Following resumption of work after a work stoppage, the company did not hire checkers to mark off lumber on three ships. The union claimed they should have been hired, the employer contended not. Marking off lumber involved the separation of the lumber in the hold of the ship by using paint, chalk, string or wire to designate and segregate the lumber by lots. This facilitated the process of unloading. The loads might have been large or small, numerous or only a single load, and they might have been composed of identical or quite diverse types of lumber. The work on one ship might have taken much, little or no time, depend-ing upon the particular circumstances. It involved no special skill.

If one examines the labor contract to determine what it said about the assignment of work, one would find the checkers' contract defined the skill as follows: A checker is an employee who receives, delivers, spot checks or weighs cargo to or from marine terminals, including piers, wharves, or ships.

The longshoremen's contract designated longshore work as the loading and discharging of cargo and the performance of incidental duties related to loading and discharging. The checkers also performed duties incidental to their major assignments. But the contracts did not give specific and exclusive jurisdiction over mark-off lumber to the checkers, nor did they prohibit longshoremen from marking off lumber. This brought into play the practice between the parties and how they had interpreted the labor contracts. Examination of the practices revealed that four different types of ships carried lumber. Four practices had been used in marking off lumber on all four types of ships: (1) not marking off at all; (2) vessel personnel did the marking off; (3) longshoremen did it; and (4) checkers performed it. All four systems had been followed on all four types of ships.

The outcome of this case displays a classic example of how a company practice of being consistently inconsistent in its manner of making job assignments enabled it to preserve its freedom of managerial discretion over future examinations. The impartial umpire under this contract ruled that the past practice showed no "implied contract" that marking off lumber belonged exclusively to checkers. Sometimes they did it, sometimes longshoremen did it, sometimes, vessel personnel, and other times, no one. To prove an implied contract, it was incumbent upon the union to show a consistent and uniform practice. As the arbiter remarked, the burden of proof is always on the party which attempts to show that the agreement means more or less or differently than it states on its face. No such proof was submitted by the union in this case. So holding, he ruled that marking off lumber did not belong exclusively to checkers.[36]

Arbitrator Harry Abrahams ruled that the General American Transportation Corp. did not violate its agreement with the Steelworkers union when it eliminated the job of storeroom attendant after a reduction of a number of employees in the plant, and instituted a system of self-service in the storeroom which eliminated the need for the performance of the attendant's primary duties of issuing and receiving tools and materials. Further, the employer had distributed remaining minor duties of the storeroom attendant to other employees in other classifications. All this took place despite the presence of contract provisions which required the maintenance of local working conditions and established procedures for changing job evaluations and incentive rates. In the judgment of the arbiter, the attendant's job description and classification did not constitute a local working condition. Secondly, the labor agreement did not restrict the employer's right to eliminate unnecessary jobs and make the distribution of the few remaining duties to other classifications.[37]

Under another contract involving the Amalgamated Meat Cutters Union, the employer retained the right to direct and control plant operations and to introduce improved production methods and facilities. Having preserved such managerial discretion, the employer was held to have possessed the right to add in-truck unloading duties to other meatcutters' duties, notwithstanding the fact that truck drivers had customarily performed such unloading duties in the past. The addition of in-truck unloading duties to meatcutters did not constitute a change in working conditions, within the meaning of the agreement, but rather constituted a change in the methods of operation.

However, while the company had the right to add such duties, it did not have the right unilaterally to do so without first discussing the matter with the union and considering whether the addition of such duties called for an increase in wage rates.[38]

The Westinghouse Electric Corporation did not act in violation of its agreement with the IUE when it upgraded an available employee to fill the vacancy on a premium pay shift created by the absence of a regularly scheduled employee. However, there existed a contractual provision, Section IX, which provided the following:

> The local policies in effect at the time of this agreement with respect to overtime and night-turn adjustment for continuous shift operations and for such special groups will be incorporated in local supplements, with only such changes as are made by mutual agreement.

The parties were in sharp disagreement as to what the local policies were with respect to overtime. The contract did not otherwise limit the employer's right to make assignments by way of replacement for absent employees, except insofar as that right was lost by a local past practice. Based on the evidence at the hearing, the arbiter concluded that there had been no established practice of treating this kind of premium pay shift assignment as belonging in the same classification as the absent employee. Whenever production schedules and needs so dictated, the company had proceeded to upgrade employees from another group. Therefore, arbitrator Nathan Cayton ruled in favor of the employer that it had not violated the labor agreement, nor any local past practice.[39]

The practice at a plant of the Mead Corporation had been to restrict female employees to jobs specified in earlier discussions and agreements between the parties. So, when District 50 of the United Mine Workers Union contested a company denial of a female employee to bump a male employee from a job in the plant that women had not previously held, arbitrator A.R. Marshall considered such prior discussions and agreements as constituting a mutual agreement between the parties. Compelling consideration was given to the fact that the union had gone along with this practice for a number of years and made no effort to establish different bumping rights for female employees during the most recent negotiations. An interesting aspect of this case was that in these recent past negotiations, the parties had introduced a clause stating that an arbitrator might consider "past practice as an aid in interpreting" the agreement if it could be shown that "such practices are in existence and have been established by mutual agreement." In view of all these circumstances, the arbiter did not feel that he could direct the employer to consider laid-off female employees for jobs held by junior male employees.[40]

The Wyandotte Chemicals Corporation had always assigned the work of replacing wooden grids to its yard department employees. On the two prior occasions when the work of converting wooden grids to ceramic tile had been done, it too had been given to these same yard department employees. When another occasion arose for this work to be performed, the employer chose to assign it to Process Department employees and its action was grieved by the Oil, Chemical and Atomic Workers union, on the premise that such work should have been assigned to yard department employees in accordance with past practice. The arbiter did not concur with the union's contentions. He acknowledged that past practice could be important and perhaps even decisive when applying provisions of a collective bargaining agreement. It also could serve to clarify and to implement contract language. However, these do not constitute its only functions. He remarked that "sometimes an established practice may, apart from any basis in the agreement, be regarded as a distinct and binding condition of employment which can only be changed by the mutual consent of the parties." It was this principle which the union was putting forth by insisting that the work assignment had in effect become a binding term of the agreement. As far as the arbitrator was concerned, this was a valid principle. However, it left unanswered the critical question as to what circumstances had to exist before such a practice might by implication become an integral part of the contract. On this point, the arbitrator made the following comment.

> The union seems to say that if a given course of conduct qualifies as a practice, it must automatically be considered a binding condition of employment. That is not so. For a practice to be enforceable, it must be supported by the mutual agreement of the parties. Its binding quality is

due not to the fact that it is past practice, but rather to the agreement
on which it is based. . . . [T]o treat all practices as binding conditions of
employment, without regard to the nature of mutuality, would be to
place past practice on an equal footing with the written agreement, a
result which the parties could hardly have contemplated.

Nothing in the record at the arbitration hearing indicated that the
practice in question was supported by mutual agreement of the parties.
Such assignments had never been the subject of negotiations or even
discussions between the parties. Even assuming that such work
assignments established a practice, in the view of the arbiter, such action
showed only the use of managerial discretion. Therefore, such practice
did not dictate that the company had to continue to exercise its discretion
in precisely the same way if the subject assignments were made. Such a
prior management practice only becomes a binding condition of employment requiring mutual consent to change when it is supported by the
mutual agreement of the parties. A situation in which the employer
merely exercised its managerial discretion as to what would be the
preferred way of performing a particular task at a particular time, could
not stand alone to produce later restrictions on its managerial
discretion.[41]

Arbitrator Arthur P. Allen considered the weight of past practice
as determinative of an employer's right to continue assigning temporary,
intermediate inspection work, estimated to average one hour a day, to
inspectors from other classifications. Under this agreement, language
provided that seniority was not controlling in the case of temporary
transfers for less than seven days. The dispute arose when an employee,
who was demoted from an intermediate inspection classification for lack
of work in that classification, grieved because the employer assigned inspectors having less seniority to perform his work for the brief period
earlier mentioned. The arbiter ruled that the grievant was not entitled to
perform intermediate inspection work whenever the volume of output
temporarily required the assignment of more intermediate inspectors.
The union had never objected to the employer's practice of making
short-term, irregular assignments, regardless of seniority. By so failing,
it, therefore, in effect had agreed that this practice was permitted under
the agreement.[42]

At the American Zinc Company, there existed a long-standing practice of assigning a helper to each skilled craftsman. Since the agreement
contained no provision requiring such assignment, arbitrator Clarence
M. Updegraff decided that the company did not need to continue such
practice. This decision was one which rested solely within management's
discretion, and, in the absence of any contractual provision to the

contrary, there was no obligation on the employer to continue such practice.[43]

No analysis of past practice could be considered complete without a review of the opinion of the late Harry Shulman, at one time the umpire between the Ford Motor Company and the UAW. Of the many remarks on this subject which may be attributed to him, none is more thought-provoking or cogent than that which appeared in one of his published decisions involving a dispute between these parties. Fortunately for the purpose of this author, Mr. Shulman's comments were produced over an issue involving an assignment of work. His comments evidence the care and caution which should be exercised by both parties, and by impartial arbitrators, when dealing with issues which involve the factor or past practice.

> A practice, whether or not fully stated in writing, may be the result of an agreement or mutual understanding. And in some industries, there are contractual provisions requiring the continuance of unnamed practices in existence at the execution of the collective agreement. (There are no such provisions in the Ford Agreement or in those of the automobile industry generally.) A practice thus based on mutual agreement may be subject to change only by mutual agreement. Its binding quality is due, however, not to the fact that it is past practice but rather to the agreement in which it is based.
>
> But there are other practices which are not the result of joint determination at all. They may be mere happenstance, that is, methods that developed without design or deliberation. Or they may be choices by Management in the exercise of managerial discretion as to the convenient methods at that time. In such cases, there is no thought of obligation or commitment for the future. Such practices are merely present ways, not prescribed ways, of doing things. The relevant item of significance is not the nature of the particular method but the managerial freedom with respect to it. Being the product of managerial determination in its permitted discretion, such practices are, in the absence of contractual provision to the contrary, subject to change in the same discretion. The law and the policy of collective bargaining may well require that the employer inform the union and that he be ready to discuss the matter with it on request. But there is no requirement of mutual agreement as a condition precedent to a change of a practice of this character.
>
> A contrary holding would place past practice on a par with written agreement and create the anomaly that, while the parties expend great energy and time in negotiating the details of the Agreement, they unknowingly and unintentionally commit themselves to unstated and perhaps more important matters which in the future may be found to have been past practice. The contrary holding would also raise other questions very difficult to answer. For example, what is properly a subject of a practice? Would the long-time use of a wheelbarrow become a practice not to be changed by the substitution of four-wheeled buggies drawn by a tow tractor? Or would the long-time use of single drill presses

be a practice prohibiting the introduction of multiple drill presses? Such restraints on technological change are alien to the automobile industry. Yet, such might be the restraints if past practice were enshrined without carefully thought out and articulated limitations. Again, when is a practice? How frequently and over how long a period must something be done before it is to be called a practice with the consequences claimed? And how is the existence of the past practice to be determined in the light of the very conflicting testimony that is common in such cases? The union's witnesses remember only the occasions on which the work was done in the manner they urge. Supervision remembers the occasions on which the work was done otherwise. Each remembers details the other does not; each is surprised at the other's perversity; and both forget or omit important circumstances. Rarely is alleged past practice clear, detailed and undisputed; commonly, inquiry into past practice of the type that is not the result of joint determination or agreement produces immersion in a bog of contradictions, fragments, doubts, and one-sided views. All this is not to say that past practice may not be important and even decisive in applying provisions of the agreement. The discussion is addressed to the different claim that, apart from any basis in the agreement, a method of operation or assignment employed in the past may not be changed except by mutual agreement.[44]

Umpire Shulman's decision in this case was that the Ford Motor Company, in spite of a practice it had followed of assigning certain work to one group of craft employees rather than to another, was not precluded from subsequently requiring a second group to perform such work. His award was premised on the factors that (1) the past practice was not based on any agreement between the parties but was one which had been unilaterally determined by the company; and (2) the nature of the work was generally accepted as a duty of the craft to which it had been subsequently assigned.

RULINGS IN FAVOR OF THE UNION

The agreement between the United States Steel Corporation and the Steelworkers union contained a provision requiring the maintenance of established local working conditions. Because of this contractual requirement, the company was held to have been in violation when it reduced its tin finishing maintenance crews by one millwright and one motor inspector for two- and three-line operations. This was so based on a 10-year practice of maintaining crews of rotating maintenance personnel of specific minimum numbers in direct relationship to the number of lines it operated. In the opinion of arbitrator Peter Florey, the assigning of certain minimun maintenance crew sizes could and did become a protected local working condition.[45]

As mentioned before, for a management action to take the form of a guiding past practice, the element of mutuality of agreement has to be present. Once this element of mutuality is part and parcel of the practice, the employer sacrifices its ability to unilaterally change the practice. This accounts for the downfall of the National Lead Company in its dispute with the Brotherhood of Painters, Decorators and Paper Hangers over a unilateral change in the duties of certain job classifications. In the agreement between the parties, a contractual provision stated, "It is not intended that the company will disregard the past practice or the language of the contract in changing, amending, modifying, or altering jobs." Secondly, a prior memorandum agreement between the parties defined the duties of the particular classifications which were involved. Such a memorandum agreement was not a unilateral act of the company, but was in fact an agreement reflecting mutuality with respect to the staffing of the particular department. An additional factor in this dispute was that there had been continuous and consistent application of the details of the agreement, and this constituted a bona fide past practice. This had become a part of the overall working contract between the parties. Based on these findings, arbitrator James J. Willingham directed the company to rescind its unilateral changes in the job content of the disputed job classifications.[46]

Under a contract between the Diamond Alkali Company and District 50 of the United Mine Workers Union, Article XVI, Section 1, provided:

> There shall be no work performed by any foreman except prior practices performed by foremen that hourly paid employees are capable of performing. This shall include all work to be performed on any day during the week. When an emergency arises, hourly paid employees shall be called to perform such work. As near as possible, this extra work shall be divided between the employees performing a similar class of work.

A dispute arose when the union contended that under this contractual clause, and on the basis of past practice in the plant, all extra work on any job had been and should be assigned to employees in the same job classification. Therefore, the union alleged that the company was in violation when it assigned a Sunday shift in a given classification to an employee from another classification. The company argued that Article XVI was not applicable as no emergency had existed. Therefore, it had the right to assign any capable employee to do the work.

In the judgment of arbitrator Dudley E. Whiting, the latter phrase of Article XVI was not equivalent to employees in the same job classification since more than one classification of jobs might be performing similar work. It was true that this situation did not involve any emergency, and there was no attempt to have a supervisor perform any duties of any hourly rated employee—so those contractual provisions were not applicable.

However, it was undisputed that a clearly established practice existed in the factory of dividing extra work among employees in the same job classifications. Faced with this consideration, arbiter Whiting ruled that "a long-existed practice or custom is an established working condition just as regular plant rules or contractual provisions are established working conditions. Such practices or customs may be changed but not without notice any more than a plant rule can be validly changed without notice." Thus he ruled that under the established practice, the grievant had been entitled to work the Sunday shift and therefore was further entitled to eight hours' pay at double time his rate of pay.[47]

Seniority

Seniority clauses in labor agreements constitute one of the areas imposing the most severe restrictions and requirements on the managing of the enterprise. Few other contractual areas so extremely and regularly interfere with a company's discretionary powers. Unless otherwise defined, and it typically is contractually defined by the parties, seniority is generally understood to mean "the length of service with the employer or in some department, section or division of the organization."

It should be understood, however, that "seniority is a relationship between employees in the same seniority unit rather than a relationship between jobs."[48]

Seniority "means that men retain their jobs according to their length of service with their employer and that men are promoted to better jobs on the same basis."[49]

Seniority issues in arbitration arise out of the attempt by the parties to promote their respective special interests.

RULINGS IN FAVOR OF THE EMPLOYER

A review of published arbitration decisions readily discloses to the researcher the fact that the parties frequently experience differences with regard to workers' seniority rights. This must be considered a type of issue which brings the parties into conflict second in frequency only to disputes involving discipline and discharge imposed by the company upon its employees. This is perhaps an easily understood and explainable consequence. To the majority of industrial workers, seniority rights represent their one real insurance of security. Under most labor agreements, it is through the exercise of seniority rights that workers retain employment or obtain it again after layoff, are promoted to more rewarding occupations, acquire preferred hours of work, and obtain more challenging tasks in which their skills and ability can be enhanced and increased. It is little wonder that workers vigorously contest any decisions or actions which may threaten these rights. Therefore, there is no shortage of these cases available for examination. Despite this abundance, only a select few have been chosen which are representative of seniority issues in which past practice played some part in affecting the ultimate outcome of the arbitral decision.

The problem between the Gas Service Company of Kansas City, Missouri, and the United Mine Workers involved a question of whether management might assign the grievant, a working foreman, and his crew to do leak survey and repair work when his predecessor, whose job the grievant had bid for successfully, had been doing new services installation work, a type of work which he expected to do when he bid the job. The union contended that the grievant's seniority entitled him to the particular work he preferred. However, nothing in the labor agreement indicated that seniority was intended to confer upon employees the right to their preference of work within their job classifications. In the absence of contract ambiguity on this point, arbitrator Marion Beatty disregarded the employer's practice of acceding to employee requests of this nature on some occasions in the past. The granting of such privileges by the company did not, under these circumstances, constitute a binding past practice on the employer.[50]

At the U.S. Rubber Company, the United Textile Workers union contested the right of the company to transfer a junior employee to a new department, rather than a senior employee who had been laid off from the old department. The union claimed a past practice existed of allowing senior employees to claim jobs in other departments when machinery had been transferred between departments. However, its contention was not established by the evidence of only two instances in which the practice was claimed to have been followed. First of all, this agreement was explicit in providing for departmental seniority. Another consideration in the opinion of this arbitrator was that the two cited instances could not be construed as constituting a continued course of conduct which amounted to a modification of the contract. As a matter of fact, the instances referred to by the union dealt with special arrangements under particular situations. Last but not least, all of the parties' prior conduct had demonstrated that they modified the contract only by formally executed bilateral agreements.[51]

The collective bargaining agreement between the Ohio Valley Gas Company and the Utility Workers union required that "in case of job vacancies, such vacancy will be posted on the bulletin board within three days." When the employer failed to post a vacancy in the job of gang foreman after the incumbent on this job had bid into a lower-rated job, the union filed a grievance. Under the management's rights article of this contract, the company had the right to make its own determination as to when a vacancy existed. Also, by agreement, the company had the unilateral right to eliminate any job for reasons of lack of work. Finally, on many prior occasions after jobs had been vacated, the employer had failed to make job postings for these vacancies without any grievance from the union. Therefore, the employer's right to use its managerial discretion not to post the job in this case was inherent in the contractual provision.[52]

It is not uncommon for management to use its hourly working forces as a source from which persons are selected for promotion into supervisory positions. This must be considered as a desirable procedure which serves to mutually benefit the hourly working force as well as the management. Such promotions are not without certain potential and intrinsic problems, however, not the least of which is the inevitable question, when a supervisor must be returned to the bargaining unit for one reason or another, as to what seniority rights he has retained or accumulated during his absence from the unit. This is a common problem which has frequently appeared before labor arbitrators, and typical is the case between the Ingersoll-Humphries Division of Borg-Warner Corp., and the International Union of Electrical Workers (IUE). In this dispute, it was the union's contention that foremen, being supervisory employees, were expressly excluded from the provisions of the contract. It was the position of the company that the foreman in question, who had been promoted from the bargaining unit, had retained and accumulated his seniority while he was a foreman and hence was entitled to bump a junior employee upon his return to the bargaining unit. Past practice proved to be determinative of the dispute. In the judgment of arbitrator Robert D. Mishne, past practice provided an interpretive force, in the absence of expressed contract language covering the situation, to bring foremen within the contract's seniority provisions. Despite the fact that foremen were excluded in general terms from coverage under the agreement, it was abundantly clear from evidence at the hearing that the company had engaged in open, notorious and repeated practices of returning foremen to the bargaining unit with retained and accumulated seniority. When the union was unable to explain its repeated failures to contest such a practice, it in effect acquiesced to the force of the practice.[53]

As mentioned, a great many cases of this type are available for review. Arbitrator Samuel S. Kates did an exceptionally fine job of reviewing such published decisions while handling such a case himself.[54] Arbiter Kates divided such cases into two general categories: (1) the earlier cases where the overwhelming number ruled that an employee's seniority is not broken by promotion so providing; and (2) the more recent cases which permit the retention, but deny the accumulation, of seniority in these situations.

Of all of the benefits derived by employees from a labor agreement, nothing could be considered as possessing more of the essence of the contract than seniority and its attendant job security. Realizing such is the case, no other consideration could more dramatically emphasize the powerful and compelling force that past practice may wield between the parties than to see it accorded such substantial effect as it was given in the case at Borg-Warner.

RULINGS IN FAVOR OF THE UNION

The International Brotherhood of Boiler Makers contended that Combustion Engineering, Inc., was obligated to apply seniority considerations in selecting employees to work through a vacation shutdown, during which only one-half of the employees were on vacation. The employer argued that seniority had not been applied during shutdowns in prior years and this constituted a past practice which should govern the outcome of the dispute. Because the contract provided for application of seniority in layoffs, and since this cessation of work fell within the definition of layoff, arbitrator William P. Murphy could not concur with the company's position. First, the union had obviously failed to acquiesce in this practice, and secondly, the contract language was viewed by him as unambiguous.[55]

Another agreement called for the employer to post any vacancy which occurred "in any job within the bargaining unit." A dispute arose when the employer claimed that it was not so obligated, citing a past practice where it had filled the last 40 such jobs over a period of more than five years, without any job postings and without complaints from the union. The particular job in question was that of working group leaders. Since these jobs were within the bargaining unit, the arbiter, faced with the unambiguous contract language, could not agree that such past practice was controlling in the absence of mutual agreement. There was no express mutual agreement that the selection of group leaders was a management prerogative. Neither could such be implied since the great majority of the instances of jobs filled by the company appeared to have involved temporary vacancies. Also, the criteria upon which the company stated it relied in making its selections were among the relevant factors which were considered in filling other jobs under the agreement. So, it was ruled that postings for these jobs were contractually required.[56]

Seniority is often exercised by employees under labor agreements in obtaining more preferred hours of work. Under a labor agreement which stated that "seniority is a principle of employment which gives preference to one employee over another based on length of continuous service," an arbiter held that the company did not have the right to discontinue an established practice of granting shift preference to senior employees at a time when it instituted a new and more efficient method of shift scheduling. Applying seniority to shift preferences was not precluded by the absence of the mention of shift preferences in the specific situations listed in the contract as requiring the application of seniority. The language of this agreement allowed the union's inquiry as to the practice followed by the parties in according such recognition to seniority.[57]

Arbitrator A.R. Marshall was another decisionmaker forced to wrestle with the question of seniority rights of employees promoted to supervisory jobs outside the bargaining unit. The contract between Republic Steel Corporation and the International Union of Mine, Mill and Smelter Workers, which was silent on this point, was interpreted herein to permit such employees to retain or accumulate seniority. The evidence indicated that it was an established practice at another plant of the employer, which operated under the same agreement, not to permit the retention or accumulation of seniority by supervisors following promotion outside of the bargaining unit. Also of consequence was that such practice had been followed in one prior instance at the plant in question.[58]

The Bethlehem Steel Company claimed an established practice of recalling employees on the basis of their regular shift assignment. However, its agreement with the Industrial Union of Marine and Shipbuilding Workers did not contain such provision and evidence did not support the company's past practice contentions. Therefore, since the agreement required that employees be recalled from layoff in inverse order of seniority, a senior employee was entitled to be recalled on the first day the plant resumed operation, even though he had regularly worked on the first shift and the first shift did not begin working until a day later.

Another interesting aspect of this case was that the employer raised a threshold issue contending the union had waived its rights to arbitration by failing to prosecute two prior similar grievances to arbitration.

Arbitrator I. Robert Feinberg did not construe this union failure to mean that it had thereby accepted the company's interpretation of the seniority provision. Commenting in this connection, he made the following remark.

> It cannot be assumed that the failure to prosecute a grievance to arbitration in two cases, any more than a failure to file a grievance in any cases, is an affirmation of the company interpretation of the contract, binding upon the union in all future cases.[59]

Another employer's admitted practice of providing seniority preferences in opportunities for overtime work were ruled by an arbiter to obligate the employer to follow seniority sequence, as far as was practicable, when it offered an overtime assignment which was not desired by those at the top of the seniority list. Thus ruling, the arbitrator required the company to compensate the third man on a seniority list for a lost overtime work opportunity which the most senior man had declined and the second most senior man would not have accepted if it had been offered to him.[60]

Hours of Work

Arbitrator Dudley E. Whiting has declared the general rule to be that "a company is free to operate its plant and direct the work of its employees in any manner not prohibited by law or by the employment or collective bargaining agreement."[61] A whole host of professional arbiters are in accord with this principle.

The matter becomes much more complex and confused when the labor agreement contains language which is ambiguous or susceptible to more than a single interpretation and is coupled with a past practice, or the contract is silent on hours of work and a plant practice is involved.

RULINGS IN FAVOR OF THE EMPLOYER

At the W.O. Larson Foundry Company, the past practice had been for employees to fill out their own time cards and retain them on their person or in their tool boxes. Under this labor agreement which stated that "employees are required to record their hours worked on time cards provided at the time clock," arbitrator Samuel S. Kates decided that the company had the right to change the form of the time card and require employees to record times for starting and ending all jobs and the time taken for specific operations performed on larger jobs. He also agreed that supervisors could indicate on employees' time cards the amount of time in which the employer expected an operation to be done, and further permitted the company to require employees to keep their time cards in the time racks at all times.[62]

The collective bargaining agreement at the Gulf Oil Corp. stated that the employer had the right "to make such changes in work schedules from time to time as it may consider necessary to the proper operation of its business." The past practice at this particular plant had been not to include Sunday in the regular work week. However, after increased traffic in the area made regular Sunday deliveries to customers necessary, the employer scheduled its gasoline delivery drivers to work on Sunday as part of their regular work week. Holding for the employer, arbitrator Sidney L. Cahn held that in the absence of some express contractual limitation, the company had the right to eliminate the past practice where the conditions upon which this past practice had been based were changed or eliminated.[63]

At the B.F. Goodrich Chemical Company, it had negotiated a labor agreement which provided pay at two and one-half the base rates for holiday work. Subsequent to entering the contract containing this provision, the employer discontinued its prior practice of working full schedules on holidays. The contract recognized that all employees would not be scheduled to work on holidays since it provided pay to employees for unworked holidays. Secondly, the general premise behind the negotiation of penalty pay provisions for holiday work is that it is designed to minimize scheduling of holiday work. Based on these considerations, arbitrator Carl A. Warns, Jr., awarded that the employer was within its rights in changing the prior work practice.[64]

Where contract language is ambiguous, past practice is often decisive on questions of contract interpretation. District 50 of the United Mine Workers challenged the interpretation of the Koppers Company of contract provisions relating to pay for short-term call-outs. Short-term call-outs were considered those with less than eight hours' advance notice. The company's interpretation that pay at time and one-half was not required for work on short-term call-out shifts, merely because the employee received less than eight hours' advance notice, nor for work on shifts following such call-outs, was accepted by arbitrator B. Meredith Reid. He so ruled where the company's interpretation conformed to the practice followed under previous contracts which contained basically the same language. A second consideration was that the union had proposed during collective bargaining of this prior contract that language be inserted spelling out the interpretation, which the union forwarded for adoption in the arbitration hearing.[65]

RULINGS IN FAVOR OF THE UNION

For 10 years, employees in the dye casting department at the Cannon Electric Company had begun and ended an hour earlier than those in other departments. The contract made no exception for them and further stated that the employer retained all rights "except as may be limited by an express provision of this agreement." The contract further specified that any departure from contractual schedules had to be by mutual agreement. When the employer unilaterally changed the shift schedules in the dye casting department to conform with schedules of other departments and shift hours set forth in the contract, the United Automobile Workers (UAW) grieved and arbitrated. In resolving the dispute, arbitrator Frederic Meyers held that the nonconforming schedules of the dye casting department could not be regarded as a "unilaterally extended privilege" on the part of the company. Since the contract stated that mutual agreement was required, it had to be presumed that a mutual agreement regarding the dye casting department operation had existed for the entire 10-year period.[66]

For many years, employees at the Cooper-Bessemer Corporation had received a 20-minute paid lunch period on the second shift when the operation was running continuous shifts. However, when continuous shift operations were stopped, the practice was not discontinued and, naturally, employees reasonably came to expect that it would be continued permanently. They viewed it as a working condition of the shift. When the company attempted to eliminate unilaterally the practice of providing a 20-minute paid period, and scheduled an unpaid lunch period, the International Association of Machinists grieved, contending that the employer was bound by the long, well-established past practice. Arbitrator Vernon L. Stouffer sustained and upheld the union's position and required the employer to restore the paid lunch period at the earliest practicable date.[67]

Following the negotiation of an agreement in which regular part-time employees who worked 25 hours or more a week were granted vacation benefits, an employer attempted to restrict the working hours of such employees to less than 25 hours per week. The Retail Clerks union argued that the Kroger Company no longer possessed the right to take such action, based on a practice of assigning such employees to 25 or more hours a week, which had been in existence for a reasonable period of time. The arbiter concurred that the parties must have negotiated their agreement based on an assumption that the practice would continue. He ruled that the employer was bound by this practice until it accomplished a change through collective bargaining with the union.[68]

Union Representatives

Dealing with union representatives in a fair, effective and equitable manner is one of management's most trying tasks. The relationship is basically adversarial and conflict is commonplace, and always potentially volatile. When the rights and privileges of the union's representatives are clearly and unambiguously spelled out in the contract, differences between the parties are less likely to grow out of proportion. When they are not, the role of past practice can be a most important element in any arbitral conclusions.

RULINGS IN FAVOR OF THE EMPLOYER

Most commonly, when past practice is a factor in an issue, the dispute involves the union's attempt to obtain, or possibly continue, some benefit or pay practice. The problems customarily revolve around the question of the union representatives' right to receive payment for time spent on union business during working hours, to enjoy freedom and latitude in the pursuit of their union activities, or some extraseniority benefit under the agreement. The following constitutes a representative sampling of disputes dealing with union representatives which appear most often in published arbitration decisions.

At the Bethlehem Steel Company, the company docked a one-half hour's pay from the wages of a union shop steward who left his machine shop at 1:00 P.M. but did not punch out his time card until 1:30 P.M., after washing up and changing to his street clothes. The Steelworkers union protested on the basis that some foremen had allowed certain union representatives to punch out in street clothes when leaving the shift early. However, such a practice did not establish a protected "local working condition" under this contract, since the union was unable to establish such supervisory treatment as a uniform and consistent behavior on the part of the majority of supervisors and employees. Such consistency and uniformity were needed in order to create an enforceable working condition which was not otherwise raised in the party's agreement. So, despite the fact that the company's policy had not been strictly enforced, arbitrator Alexander B. Porter upheld the company's position.[69]

In another case, the Philco Corporation advised the International Union of Electrical Workers (IUE), prior to the union's election of officers, that it was going to stop paying union officials for time spent in committee meetings and other time spent processing and handling grievances. Although this action was not upheld by an arbitral ruling finding such union officials entitled to pay for time thus spent to the expiration date of the then-current agreement, such payment was not required after the effective date of the subsequent contract where no provision for such pay was included. The union's failure to negotiate a contractual provision which continued this practice resulted in a termination of the company's obligation. In the view of arbitrator Lawrence E. Seibel, such payments did not relate to union officials' employment as employees of the company. Therefore, company pay for time spent processing and handling grievances did not constitute a term or condition of employment that could be modified only through collective bargaining. Once the employer had given notice of its intent to terminate the practice, it could do so upon termination of the existing contract.[70]

The International Association of Machinists (IAM) claimed a right to be paid by the company for time spent at arbitration hearings. It pointed to two situations in which union representatives were paid for time so spent. Arbitrator Clarence M. Updegraff did not agree. The contract merely stated that union representatives would be paid for time spent in "negotiations," "meetings," and "conferences" with the employer. Therefore, since the employer established that the two instances cited were the result of misunderstandings by subordinate representatives of the company, and since the agreement did not require such payments, the arbiter interpreted the agreement as requiring pay only for business meetings that did occur routinely and frequently from time to time as the parties sought by discussion and agreement to dispose of problems which arose between them.[71]

Under another agreement, the practice in the past had been to grant permission to union representatives to use the company's conference rooms for discussions. When the employer refused to continue this practice, the union grieved and arbitrated. The arbitrator could not find the employer's action as a violation of the contract since the agreement was silent on this matter, and the practice of granting permission had been unilaterally established by the company and therefore might also be unilaterally withdrawn.[72]

The contract between Armour and Company and the United Packinghouse Workers of America required continuance of "local working conditions agreed to by local collective bargaining." This language did not require the company to continue a 10-year local practice of permitting the distribution of union literature during nonworking time where such practice had never been made a part of any local agreement.[73]

RULINGS IN FAVOR OF THE UNION

Mentioned earlier was a dispute between two parties in which the union had claimed that the company was obliged to pay for the time of union officials spent at arbitration hearings. Their contention in that case was based on the premise that the employer had made such payments on two prior occasions. In that dispute, those two prior instances were insufficient to constitute a practice. Secondly, the employer was able to establish that such payments had erroneously been made by subordinate management representatives. A different outcome resulted in the following case when the weight and force of past practice were substantially compelling. This agreement required the company to pay shop stewards, local union officers, and aggrieved employees for such time as they may lose from their regular shift in order to attend scheduled meetings on grievances with employer representatives. The employer contended that "meetings on grievances" did not include arbitration hearings. However, this interpretation as urged by the employer was rejected by the arbitrator in view of the company's consistent past practice, spanning a period of several years and several contracts, of paying union representatives for their attendance at arbitration hearings. Therefore, he ruled that the employer was obliged to pay stewards, union officials and aggrieved employees for time spent at arbitration hearings consistent with that prior custom.[74]

Also previously mentioned under "Rulings in Favor of the Employer" were cases where arbitrators did not require employers to pay union representatives for time spent in handling grievances. Again, the outcome of any given case can be materially affected if the union is able to establish, to the satisfaction of the arbiter, that such payments have been made for a substantial period of time.

Arbitrator Harry J. Dworkin ruled that the Industrial Rayon Corporation was obligated to continue its practice of paying employees for time spent as union officials in processing grievances, even though there was no contractual provision expressly requiring such grievance payments. The Textile Workers union was able to clearly establish hat such payment had been made for at least 15 years. In the judgment of the arbiter, such payments had become a condition of employment which could not unilaterally be abolished during the life of the agreement. The one concession granted by the arbiter was that the employer was not precluded from exercising some reasonable controls to guard against abuse and unnecessarily excessive costs.[75]

Overtime

It is a fairly well-established arbitral conclusion that management can require employees to perform a reasonable amount of work beyond their regular hours of work, if there is no contractual provision providing otherwise. Regrettably, the scheduling of overtime by supervisors is the contractual area in which the greatest differences in administration and implementation occur. It seems that, typically, foremen from a particular department experience unique and peculiar overtime problems, which provoke them to schedule overtime, select employees, etc., in a manner different from other departments, thus raising the specter of conflicting practices. This is merely one area of past practice disputes; many others follow herein.

RULINGS IN FAVOR OF THE EMPLOYER

At the Morton Salt Company, the International Chemical Workers union posited that a past practice required the company to pay for time not worked when there had been some error in overtime distribution which should have been rectified. The union further contended that the company had, without objection, accepted and processed a series of overtime pay grievances which amounted to acquiescence by the company to the union's interpretation of the contractual overtime provisions. When arbitrator Paul M. Hebert was unable to find to his satisfaction the existence of such established practices, he ruled that the employer could remedy an erroneous overtime assignment by offering to the aggrieved employee an overtime assignment at a time of choice, within a designated period, on work that would not otherwise have been performed at overtime rates. The only proviso was that the erroneous assignment had to occur within the group of employees eligible for overtime. He considered such remedy appropriate for the reasons that (1) such approach would not deprive other employees of overtime work; and (2) the employer thus incurred a monetary penalty that it would not have incurred except for its error; and (3) it also gave the employee a fair and equitable remedy. A feature of this award (satisfying to the employer but unpleasant to the union) was that the employee thus had to perform some work for the employer before he received the monetary remedy.[76]

In connection with the above award, perhaps a comment may be in order. Certainly, the remedy fashioned by the arbitrator appeared to be a fair and reasonable one which brought a degree of equity to the situation for all parties. The employer experienced the penalty for its erroneous judgment in overtime distribution; the aggrieved employee was provided with an opportunity to receive the overtime payment which he had been wrongfully denied; and in so accomplishing this remedy, no other employee was caused to sacrifice future overtime to which he might be entitled. For these reasons, the following re marks are certainly not intended in any way to constitute a negative reflection upon the merits of this decision. Under the facts and circumstances of that case, the award appears to have been perfectly reasonable and proper. It is perhaps somewhat untypical from the majority of arbitration decisions dealing with erroneous overtime assignments by the employer. In the majority of cases, where the company is deemed to have judged improperly in employee selections for overtime, decisions appear to support the premise that an overtime payment is required by the employer for which he receives no work performed. The basic concept endorsed by many is that overtime represents a period of time in the life of the parties to the agreement, which is available only once at the time it occurs, and once gone is lost forever, never to be recaptured.

In other words, if an employer improperly assigns a four-hour overtime period to the wrong employee, if it provides the remedy of four hours' work to the right employee at some future time, it will be providing work to the grievant which actually should then be assigned to another employee. Therefore, by taking corrective action and providing four hours' work to the grievant, it in effect denies a work opportunity on an overtime basis to another employee who would have otherwise worked. The initial four-hour overtime period is available to the parties but once, and that is at the precise four-hour time period in which it occurs. Following this rationale, many arbiters have required the employer to make payments for the lost overtime at appropriate rates rather than require him to give employees future overtime work opportunities.

Where a labor agreement established no starting time for the work day, but provided for continuance of any prior practices not in conflict with the agreement, the company's consistent practice had been to start the work day for all employees at 8:00 A.M. This contract further required that the employer make a double-time payment to an employee who worked his regular shift from 4:00 P.M. to midnight on Tuesday, and was off until he was called in at noon on Friday, four hours ahead of his regular shift. He was deemed by an arbiter not to be entitled to double-time pay for the hours from noon to 4:00 P.M. on Friday. He refused to rule that the employer violated the labor agreement when it deemed that the employee's second day off ended at 8:00 A.M. on Friday.[77]

RULINGS IN FAVOR OF THE UNION

In a case involving Carnegie Illinois Steel Corporation and the Steelworkers union, the employer supplied evidence of a long-term practice of not counting as days worked for premium pay purposes, holidays on which employees were absent. The union claimed that contrary language existed which was unambiguous and unqualified. The arbiter made the following comment.

> We clearly cannot apply practices which are in direct conflict with that agreement, without in effect, altering and even nullifying the agreement itself.[78]

The Celanese Fibers Company did not have a right to eliminate its practice of instructing employees in fire fighting on overtime. It had attempted to schedule such fire fighting instruction during the regular work week at straight time rates. However, District 50 of the United Mine Workers presented evidence of a clearly established practice which had been continued and rigidly adhered to for more than 10 years. Based on this consideration, the arbiter disallowed the unilateral discontinuance of the practice and held that it could be changed only by the parties in collective bargaining.[79]

The following case represents an example of a dispute where a long-established practice carried more compelling force than clear contract language. In this instance, the parties adopted the disputed contractual provision without any real discussion regarding it, and there was evidence which indicated that the provision was modeled after another contract which had been used as a sample, and neither party really understood what the provision meant. Further evidence of this conclusion was that the company continued its prior practice for a month after the contract was executed. This further indicated that the parties had probably not agreed to any change in the prior practice. Therefore, the employer was required to continue its precontract practice of counting daily unpaid lunch periods as time worked for the purpose of computing overtime worked by employees. This was the arbitral ruling even though the contested contract language stated that "eight consecutive hours in a regular work shift, exclusive of a lunch period, shall constitute a normal day's work."[80]

5. Standards Determining a Fixed and Established Past Practice

Maybe it's futile to attempt to identify any standards by which arbitrators determine if a practice exists which should be given some weight and effect in their decision. The more one investigates the many published decisions where past practice has been involved, the easier it is to form the conclusion that there is no unanimity of opinion among arbiters as to precise standards. The easiest conclusion to reach is that the decision reached in any particular case is greatly dependent upon the individual thinking of the particular arbitrator deciding the issue. Archibald Cox once made the following statement:

> Outside the areas controlled by statute, there is no more important treasury of experience than the record of grievance arbitration. Surely arbitrators have not labored at the administration of collective bargaining agreements for almost two decades without arriving at some generalization upon which the unbiased can agree, even though partisan interests preclude unanimity.[1]

It must be considered true that many practitioners representing labor and management have found some guiding generalizations in arbitral opinion which have provided some expectant and predictable outcomes on certain issues. But those practitioners engaged in such searches must certainly be somewhat disappointed when it comes to the question of past practice. The best that can be said here is that there are only uncertain generalizations and no indisputable rules.

Now that this has been said, an attempt will be made, which may prove to be merely a feeble one, to provide some idea of the type of standards generally utilized by the majority of arbitrators. Perhaps, in retrospect, it will be considered an effort that went for naught, but it is better to have made the attempt and failed than not to have made the attempt at all.

I believe that the majority of arbitration decisions involving past practice, where such practice or custom was given some influential weight in the final outcome, contained one or more of the following four ingredients. Conversely, where the party pressing for compelling consideration of past practice failed to establish that one or more of these same ingredients existed, the award went to the other party. To give support to this contention, arbitration cases have been supplied in which such ingredients were pertinent to the arbiter's solution.

1. Unequivocal That is to say, the practice has been granted or applied consistently, uniformly, regularly and without break.

2. Clearly Enunciated This means that the practice has been acquiesced in by the parties and has operated without protest or objection from one party or the other.

3. Duration It has existed and been followed over a reasonably long period of time. In this regard, as will be shown, a bridge effect may be of significance to some arbitrators. The bridge effect results from a practice commencing under one agreement and continuing unchanged and unprotested into a renewed agreement. Thus, it bridges the collective bargaining negotiations between the parties without having been changed or discontinued. It should also be noted that the frequency of the practice may not be as consequential as the consistency of its application. In other words, a practice which occurs only three times a year in which on each occasion the practice is consistently executed, may conceivably have more weight and effect than another practice which occurs fifteen times a year, but is inconsistently administered from one time to another.

4. Jointly Accepted and Acted Upon This means that both parties, through their line representatives, have operated as though the practice in fact existed and was a guiding rule. This may signify to some arbitrators a mutuality aspect which then conceivably makes the practice one resulting from bilateral action as opposed to unilateral action.

Let us turn now to case examples where these factors were influential. Arbitrator Whitley P. McCoy, serving as chairman of a tripartite board for Kaiser Aluminum and Chemical Corporation and the Aluminum Workers International Union, ruled in favor of a binding past practice in a call-in pay dispute. In view of the practice, employees who completed their regular 8:00 A.M. to 4:00 P.M. shift on one day, and were then called and told to report early on the following day, were not entitled to four hours' pay for time worked prior to 8:00 A.M. on the second day, even though the contract provided (1) that the work day was from 8:00 A.M. to 8:00 A.M., and (2) that employees called in to work on the second shift within the same work day should be paid for not less than four hours' work.

Three features — uniformity, acquiescence by the parties, and long-continued existence — were all present and influenced the decision.

The company proved that a uniform practice has existed, where the man called out has continued to work on into his regular shift, to count the time on his regular shift in computing the minimum of four hours paid for. An employee of the company's payroll department testified that so far as he knew payment had always been made as it was made in this case, when a man called out continued working into his regular shift. He testified that he had made a random check and had been unable to find any instance of paying allowed time under the circumstances. Other supervisors testified as to instances that they recalled where payment had been made in the same manner as in this case. They testified as to these instances, giving names and circumstances. The union offered no evidence of an instance where payment had been made in accordance with its interpretation of this contract section.

Uniform and long-continued practice, known to and concurred in by both parties, is of course good evidence as to the intent placed upon contract language by the parties.[2]

As mentioned earlier, a practice may be deemed as possessing compelling weight even though it may occur relatively infrequently, if it is regularly and consistently applied in a given fashion. Such was the case in a dispute resolved by arbitrator Hubert C. Callaghan for the North American Cement Corporation and the United Cement, Lime and Gypsum Workers. The arbiter ruled that evidence of four instances over a period of eight and one-half years was sufficient to establish a practice of filling job vacancies by lottery when two of four applicants for the vacancy had equal seniority and the minimum ability required for the job. Since the situation was necessarily one of infrequent occurrence, and, therefore, one in which a relatively small number of instances would be required to establish a practice, consistency of administration was easily and clearly established. Another element, that of acquiescence, was evident since the union heretofore had not protested. On the matter of relative infrequency of the occurrence, the arbiter posed a question which he then endeavored to answer for the parties: In labor relations, how many instances are necessary to establish a practice? Naturally, the answer will vary with the nature of the situation. If the problem is one which normally occurs fairly frequently, and is not dealt with in the contract, a relatively large number of instances might be required to establish a practice. But, if the problem is one which does not occur very frequently, such as in the instant case, a relatively small number of occurrences might be sufficient to establish a practice.[3]

The bridge effect of a practice continuing from one agreement into the next was one of the principal ingredients in a dispute resolved by Harold M. Gilden. Despite the fact that a retirement plan was unilaterally established, compulsory retirement of employees when they reached retirement age fixed by the retirement plan was ruled as proper, since the retirement plan had been in effect for a long period of time and the union had never protested against the compulsory retirement feature. In addition to the bridge effect referred to in the arbitrator's decision, the case had two features: (1) existence over a reasonably long period of time; and (2) acquiescence by the parties.

In this issue, the union attempted to do by means of arbitration what it could not accomplish during negotiations. It bargained with full knowledge of the company's retirement policy and accepted the language which appeared in the local agreements. The union, by its silence, either had abandoned its objections to the retirement program, or at least had yielded to an established management prerogative.

This was not a situation where the company attempted to inaugurate a retirement policy. The arbitrator was here presented with a tenuous claim based on an unrealistic and startling definition of the word "discharge." He was asked to rewrite a contract agreed to by the parties in the light of years of past practice and interpretation, and to throw open to dispute the resulting multitude of thorny problems.[4]

Arbitrator Edgar A. Jones also endorsed this bridge concept when he made the following remarks in a case decided by him.

> It is well accepted that a course of conduct engaged in by one party and acquiesced in by the other party to a collective bargaining agreement, spanning two or more contract terms — without any interim contractual reaction to it — becomes a part of the agreement between the parties and cannot be substantially altered or discontinued except by bilateral negotiations....[5]

Arbitrator McCoy revealed his agreement with the bridge doctrine when he stated the following in one of his many published decisions.

> The contract does not contain any provision concerning this matter. However, it could hardly be denied that plant practices and customs have existed at the time the contract was executed, bearing on working conditions and which the parties did not contemplate changing, are by implication a part of the contract....[6]

Past practice was clearly controlling in the next case. The factors of the bridge effect, acquiescence by the union without protest and long and consistent administration, were all compelling features of this controlling practice. The involved contract granted vacation pay at the employee's regular rate and defined it as the employee's regular straight time rate on the job to which he was regularly assigned at the time of becoming eligible for vacation. The employer computed the vacation pay of the aggrieved employee, who was transferred to a lower- rated job one week before vacation, on the basis of the wage rate for the lower-rated job, since the employee would have been assigned to the lower-rated job had he not taken vacation at that time. The company's long-standing practice under this agreement, without protest from the union, had been to pay for vacations at the same rate the employee would have received if he had actually been at work. There was no evidence that this disputed method of computation had been deliberately used to give an employee less vacation pay than he was entitled to receive. The pertinent remarks of arbiter Joseph M. Klamon were as follows.

> It is a universally recognized rule that in interpreting a contract clause capable of more than one meaning the intention of the parties as evidenced in long-established past practice is an important and often a controlling factor.... [W]hen a method of computing vacation pay is not challenged either in grievance procedure or during contract negotiations for many years of collective bargaining history, it is reasonable to find and to hold as we do that the past practice of the company in computing such vacation pay on the basis that it has used for many years has met with at least the implied assent of the union.... [I]f the parties wish to effect a drastic change, or spell out more specifically a different interpretation than the one clearly established and accepted by the union without protest over many years of past practice, they can only do so during the next contract negotiations or by supplemental agreement to the present contract....[7]

This case is interesting for more reasons than its revealed accord with the standards which were outlined earlier. It also discloses one of the avenues open to the parties who have become encumbered by a practice undesirable to them. Obviously, either party may find itself in this position—in this particular case, it was the union.

The specific avenue of escape suggested by the arbitrator here was for the union to bargain it out. This probably meant that the union would be waiting until the expiration of this agreement to accomplish this objective, since the company was probably satisfied with the outcome of this arbitration case. It is conceivable, however, that the union might be able to persuade the employer to engage in negotiations on this subject during the term of the agreement, provided it was willing to enter those discussions ready to grant a concession to the employer of greater consequence to the employer than this vacation decision.

Arbitrator Paul Prasow found the duration of a practice and the union's acquiesence to it to be controlling in a Proctor and Gamble case with the Proctor and Gamble Employees Association. The job of jar unpacker was ruled properly considered by the company a job within the general classification of packer. The classification of packer was one which under the contract was confined to female employees, and in its performance, jar unpacking was inherently related to, and an integral part of, the packing line. This ruling resulted despite the union's contentions that unpacking, as contrasted to packing, was unsuitable for women and the jar unpackers were not included in the contract listing of women's jobs. The governing factor was that of past practice.

> ...[I]n every instance, whenever the company indicated, by practice, that it considered and understood jar unpacker to be a woman's job and part of the packer title, the union apparently went along with this interpretation. For over two years, there was an acceptance by the union of the company's interpretation inferred by the union's conduct. It is clear that there is an acceptance where the relations of the parties, through their previous dealings or through other circumstances, are such as to impose a duty to speak, but where silence is maintained. Silence on the part of the union to a company interpretation of a clause, as practiced over the two-year period, could conceivably, in management's mind, constitute acceptance of this interpretation.[8]

In the above-cited case, the company also pointed out that the union did not raise the issue in negotiations on the new contract, which would have been the proper time for it. This they failed to do even during specific bargaining discussions regarding packing lines in the factory.

Another employer did not have the right, without the consent of the union, to discontinue its practice of granting leaves of absence to pregnant employees and to adopt instead a policy requiring the discharge of such parties when their work deteriorated or risk of injury became evident. Accordingly, an employee who was discharged under this new policy, rather than being given a leave of absence, was reinstated with back pay from the time of her discharge, except for a five-week period during which she would have been absent on leave. On the evidence presented to the arbitrator, it was clearly apparent that the granting of maternity leave was a long-established, important and known practice, not referred to in any specific contract clause. As such, the long-standing practice ripened into an integral part of the bargaining relationship and became a condition of employment which the employees and the union understandably had a reasonable expectation would continue.[9]

The scheduling of lunch periods and the impact of past practice upon management's right to change them was the question presented to arbitrator Clarence M. Updegraff by the Bake-Lite Company and the United Glass and Ceramic Workers union. On the shift of work which ran from 8:00 A.M. to 4:00 P.M., the practice had been to schedule lunch periods in four 30-minute periods between 11:00 A.M. and 1:00 P.M. The employer unilaterally changed the schedule of lunch periods to five 30-minute periods between 10:45 A.M. and 1:15 P.M. The text of the agreement contained nothing restrictive as to the time for lunch periods of shift workers. However, the union's concern was that the change in schedule placed the earliest and latest lunch periods unreasonably near the beginning and end of the shift. The changes actually caused some men to work two hours and 45 minutes before lunch and then four hours and 45 minutes after lunch. Others would work four hours and 45 minutes prior to the half-hour lunch period and then work two hours and 45 minutes thereafter. In the view of the union, if the employer could extend the lunch period by 15 minutes each way, why not 30 minutes or more at its convenience, bringing them even more unreasonably away from the mid-time of the shift. Although the agreement was silent with regard to when particular lunch periods should be scheduled, the arbiter felt that this was a case where the usage of past practice had been virtually uniform and so relied on in the past that the time for luncheon periods had to be regarded as restricted to the two-hour period from 11:00 A.M. to 1:00 P.M. theretofore scheduled, and apparently concurred in by the parties.[10] Again, we see a situation here where at least some of the above-mentioned four ingredients (page 108) were instrumental in the final results. Arbitrator Paul M. Hebert clearly stated his complete agreement with the various principles under discussion here.

> Past practice to be binding must be unequivocal, clearly enunciated and acted upon and readily ascertainable over a reasonable period of time as a fixed practice accepted by both parties. The past practice under a disputed contract provision is not controlling where the interpretation of the clause has long been the subject of dispute between the parties.[11]

Applying these principles, he decided that past practice seemed inconclusive in deciding a case that involved questions of seniority, job classifications and the filling of vacancies by the posting of jobs for bid. While the employer in this case had maintained its position that jobs in its warehouse were not subject to the bidding procedure, the union had disputed this interpretation. Furthermore, the company had permitted bidding on some jobs so that its practice of denying bids had been contaminated by its own actions.

Confusing evidence of past practice was presented to arbitrator Charles A. Reynard in a case where both parties invoked arguments of past practice to resolve an ambiguity in their contract terms. Arbiter Reynard acknowledged that where contract language is capable of yielding different interpretations, resort may be made to past practice in order to resolve the ambiguity. The difficulty here, however, was that there was no agreement upon what that past practice had been. The evidence on the point was in substantial conflict, so much so that the arbiter was not persuaded by either version. The union's evidence appeared to show that on two occasions it had protested the assignment of the challenged work and the work was stopped. The company's evidence relating to these same two incidents indicated that the work was stopped, not because of the union's protest, but because its use of the particular equipment involved was concluded in both instances. The company further presented evidence that it had performed the challenged work with the challenged equipment on several other occasions, that some of these assignments were protested by the union, but in all instances, the company rejected protests, and the union acquiesced in the assignment. Because of his inability to determine the validity of either practice, one cancelled the other, and he viewed it as his unavoidable duty to resolve the issue in terms of the burden of proof. The union, being the complaining party here, was held to have failed to sustain the burden of establishing a clear pattern of past practice to support its claim.[12]

An employer may handicap his ability to act unilaterally in imposing discipline for breach of plant rules based on some prior conduct in its administration of discipline. This happened to the Coca-Cola Bottling Company in its agreement with the International Brotherhood of Teamsters. Over a period of ten years of contractual relations between the parties, the employer had established a custom that no discharge for dishonesty was made without first giving the union the opportunity to investigate and act on its own. Finally, a dispute developed when the employer broke this custom. It failed to formally notify the union of the company's belief that an employee was guilty of theft until the very day of his discharge. In so doing, the union was accorded no opportunity to make an investigation on its own and to discuss the problem in advance with the company. By violating the established contractual custom for handling such cases, the company breached the labor agreement. Here again is a past practice, which had been unequivocal, of long duration, and one that had been accepted and acted upon by representatives of both the company and the union. As time went on, it evolved into a binding commitment by the company to proceed in strict accordance with it, or be found in violation of the contract of which it had become an integral part.[13]

Another past practice was considered as cemented into the relationship between the parties where a successor union incorporated into its first agreement with the company language which had existed in the former agreement with the predecessor union for 10 years. By bridging the negotiations and failing to raise any question about the prior interpretation of the clause, the officers and members of the new local were presumed to have been satisfied with the interpretation and operation of the particular clause. In so ruling, arbitrator Leo C. Brown charged this succeeding union with knowledge of the prior practice under the same contract language as it permitted it to appear in its first contract.[14]

Arbitrator Russell A. Smith found himself deciding a reporting (for work) pay dispute in which the union contended that on one occasion reporting pay, under the same contract provision and like circumstances, had voluntarily been paid by the employer thus establishing, by practice, the intent and meaning of the contract. Arbiter Smith could not agree that a single incident established a practice of the parties in the interpretation and application of their contract. The fact that the company had paid reporting pay under like circumstances did not, standing alone, afford an independent basis for upholding the union's grievance. As he observed, if the situation were reversed, and payment had been refused on this prior occasion, the union certainly would have been justified in contending here that, just because it failed to make a case of the one incident, it should not be precluded from making one in this instance.[15] Obviously, none of the essential ingredients could be found in this dispute.

In order for a past practice to be important in determining the meaning of language, "the practice must be of sufficient generality and duration to imply acceptance of it as an authentic construction of the contract." So holding, arbitrator Robert E. Mathews, appointed to resolve a call-in dispute, ruled that an interpretation of the contract contrary to its apparent intent was not justified by the mere showing of the practice of a few payments over an 18-month period.[16]

An arbitrator ordinarily might uphold a union's contention that a contract provision requires payment for 56 hours to an employee who works six consecutive eight-hour days beginning on Sunday, where the governing provision states that the overtime rate will be paid for Sunday work and work in excess of 40 hours per week, but that the premium will not be granted twice for the same hours. However, a long-standing practice complicated matters.

The company argued that Sunday premium was paid as daily overtime and should not be counted as a day of work for the purpose of computing weekly overtime forty (40) hours. If the overtime was figured on both a weekly and a daily basis, the company would be required to pay a premium on both a daily and a weekly basis which was greater than that required by the contract. In order to pay overtime for the sixth day of work, the company asserted it would be necessary to count the Sunday hours worked which were paid for at a premium rate, in order to pay the overtime rate on the sixth day of work. This would amount to paying overtime on the same hours worked.

Looking at the contract language alone and without regard to the bargaining history, the arbitrator might have been inclined to agree with the union's interpretation, which was that an employee who worked six 8-hour days commencing on a Sunday would be entitled to payment of fifty-six hours' pay. However, an ambiguity existed as to the proper interpretation of the contract language. The existence of the ambiguity was underscored by a 12-year bargaining history where the union involved had repeatedly sought a change in the contract wording which would have agreed with the interpretation placed upon the disputed clauses by the union. Throughout the parties' bargaining history, the company refused to make this language concession sought by the union. Also throughout their bargaining relationship of the prior 12 years, the union had lived with the company's interpretation and the past practice which developed and grew as a result of it. For these reasons, the arbitrator recognized this practice and so interpreted the ambiguous provision, deciding finally in accord with it and ruling that the company had not violated the overtime premium pay clauses.[17]

This is another supporting example of the established concept that practices growing up under one agreement are strengthened and entrenched when they survive contract negotiations between the parties and are continued unchanged and unabated into another contract term, particularly where any relevant contract provision is unclear, vague, or ambiguous. Such a continuation of like practice with readoption of identical contract language usually gives rise to the presumption that the parties intended to continue the prior practices established thereunder.

What this can mean to the respective parties under the agreement is illustrated again where a dispute centered about a contractual phrase that vacation pay should be computed on the basis of "the regularly scheduled work week," as that phrase appeared in the vacation article of the contract between the parties. The problem in this situation was between the A.O. Smith Corp. and the United Electrical, Radio and Machine Workers. The union contended that this phrase meant the regularly scheduled work week of the individual employee, or, at least, of the department. The company claimed that this phrase could mean only the regularly scheduled work week of the entire plant. Depending upon which method was used for computation, the earnings of employees could be materially affected. Naturally, the interpretation sought by the union provided a more liberal vacation pay allowance. The section in question was not as clear or well written as might have been wished, and, on its face, was ambiguous in that it might be susceptible to more than one interpretation.

Faced with this type of problem, the arbitrators did that which is commonplace to all arbitrators faced with similar controversies. Since the parties had failed to express their intent with clarity in the labor agreement, the ambiguity had to be resolved by making reference to the collective bargaining of the parties on this subject, and to any past practice which surrounded this contract clause's administration. The evidence on the record was clear and undisputed that the interpretation of the language was as the company contended—plant-wide—rather than according to the scheduled work week of the individual employee or department. Since the practice favored the company's plant-wide interpretation, and since the union was knowledgeable of this fact prior to and during the negotiations, it was the union's responsibility to alter the vacation wording to make the union's intent clear. The arbitrator made the following remarks.

> . . . [F]or in accepting the identical language, without expressing a clear change in intent, the union ran the risk of having any ambiguity in the language resolved on the basis of the contract established by the practice. . . . [A]ny party desiring a change in application or meaning must assume the responsibility of seeing to it that the wording of the provision involved is qualified or modified to make explicit the change intended.
>
> It is a well-established principle of industrial arbitration that where past practice has established a meaning for language that is subsequently used by the parties in a new agreement, the language will be presumed to have the meaning given it by past practice.[18]

The precise question before arbitrator Peter M. Kelliher had been placed before another arbitrator in a previous arbitration hearing, involving the same parties, and precisely the same contract language. The only difference in the case before arbitrator Kelliher was that the aggrieved party was different than in the prior arbitration hearing. Subsequent to the prior arbitral decision, the parties negotiated and entered a new agreement in which the same language was repeated. The allegations of the past practice put forth by the union were not denied by the company, nor was its evidence of the prior arbitration award. The arbiter had no choice but to find that on the basis of the prior award and the settled past practice, the same construction and interpretation of the labor agreement had been carried over into the new agreement.[19]

Again, we find the importance of the bridge effect to the arbitral conclusions, but in this instance supported by the additional weight of a prior arbitration award of precedential value.

Arbitrator Whitley P. McCoy was another who stated this principle in the case of Dwight Manufacturing Company and the Textile Workers of America. In this opinion, he stated the following:

Such practice, on familiar principles of law, constituted a construction of the contract by the parties themselves, and became a part of that contract by virtue of such construction. Therefore, when the identical language, thus construed by the parties, was incorporated into the latest contract, the construction was also reincorporated.[20]

One of the essential ingredients to make a practice compelling and binding is that it be acquiesced in by the parties. Even where it may meet the test of having continued for a long period of time with consistent and uniform administration, it often falls before an arbiter where either party can demonstrate its long-standing objections to the practice. Such was the case at the Hotpoint Company in its agreement with the United Auto Workers. Despite a company claim that its practices in vacation administration were long-standing, it could hardly speak of its actions as reflecting an accepted practice. The union in its early negotiations with the company, in its presentation of several grievances before an arbitrator, and in the instant case before arbitrator Otto J. Babb, had certainly and definitely objected to this so-called past practice. Therefore, although the practice had endured for a considerable period of time, it was rejected in the final analysis.[21]

My intentions in reviewing these cases has been, hopefully, to provide the reader with some general standards which may provide insights into the role of past practice in arbitral decisionmaking. Conceivably, and perhaps understandably, such an objective, at best, is very difficult to achieve. Although past practice is not the sole problem that has perplexed those in the labor-management arena, it certainly must rank high within a list that would comprise the more perplexing issues. Arbitrators' decisionmaking is actually not the mystical process that it might appear to be at first glance. Generalizations regarding the weight and effect arbiters accord to past practice are not a mythical attainment, as many practitioners in the labor relations field are sometimes prone to believe. After reading the many published cases on past practice, a natural inclination might be to fear that arbitrators make their judgments on cases involving this issue in a capricious manner. This author hopes in some small way to have dismissed the notion of this possibility from the minds of some practitioners.

Appendix A: Representative Arbitral Commentary

Custom and past practice unquestionably constitute one of the most significant factors in labor-management arbitration. Evidence of custom and past practice may be introduced for any of the following major purposes: (1) to provide the basis of rules governing matters not included in the written contract; (2) to indicate the proper interpretation of ambiguous contract language; or (3) to support allegations that clear language of the written contract has been amended by mutual action or agreement.

Some of the general statements of arbitrators in this regard, which touch upon one or more of the major purposes listed above, are found in the following rulings.

Martin M. Volz: "[I]t is well recognized that the contractual relationship between the parties normally consists of more than the written word. Day-to-day practices mutually accepted by the parties may attain the status of contractual rights and duties, particularly where they are not at variance with any written provision negotiated into the contract by the parties and where they are of long standing and were not changed during contract negotiations."[1]

Arthur T. Jacobs: "A union-management contract is far more than words on paper. It is also all the oral understandings, interpretations and mutually acceptable habits of action which have grown up around it over the course of time. Stable and peaceful relations between the parties depend upon the development of a mutually satisfactory superstructure of understanding which gives operating significance and practicality to the purely legal wording of the written contract. Peaceful relations depend, further, upon both parties faithfully living up to their mutual commitments as embodied not only in the actual contract itself but also in the modes of action which have become an integral part of it."[2]

Dallas L. Jones: "It is generally accepted that certain, but not all, clear and long standing practices can establish conditions of employment as binding as any written provision of the agreement."[3]

Whitley P. McCoy: "But caution must be exercised in reading into contracts implied terms, lest arbitrators start re-making the contracts which the parties have themselves made. The mere failure of the Company, over a long period of time, to exercise a legitimate function of management, is not a surrender of the right to start exercising such right. If a Company had never, in 15 years and under 15 contracts, disciplined an employee for tardiness, could it thereby be contended that the Company could not decide to institute a reasonable system of penalties for tardiness? Mere non-use of a right does not entail a loss of it."[4]

Whitley P. McCoy: "Custom can, under some circumstances, form an implied term of a contract. Where the Company has always done a certain thing, and the matter is so well understood and taken for granted that it may be said that the contract was entered into upon the assumption that that customary action would continue to be taken, such customary action may be an implied term."[5]

Maurice H. Merrill: "In the light of the [arbitration] decisions,... it seems to me that the current of opinion has set strongly in favor of the position that existing practices, in respect to major conditions of employment, are to be regarded as included within a collective bargaining contract, negotiated after the practice has become established and not repudiated or limited by it. This also seems to me the reasonable view, since the negotiators work within the frame of existent practice and must be taken to be conscious of it."[6]

Richard Mittenthal: "Consider first a practice which is, apart from any basis in the agreement, an enforceable condition of employment on the theory that the agreement subsumes the continuance of existing conditions. Such a practice cannot be unilaterally changed during the life of the agreement. For ... if a practice is not discussed during negotiations most of us are likely to infer that the agreement was executed on the assumption that the practice would remain in effect.

"That inference is based largely on the parties' acquiescence in the practice. If either side should, during the negotiation of a later agreement, object to the continuance of this practice, it could not be inferred from the signing of a new agreement that the parties intended the practice to remain in force. Without their acquiescence, the practice would no longer be a binding condition of employment. In face of a timely repudiation of a practice by one party, the other must have the practice written into the agreement if it is to continue to be binding."[7]

Jules J. Justin: "Plain and unambiguous words are undisputed facts. The conduct of Parties may be used to fix a meaning to words and phrases of uncertain meaning. Prior acts cannot be used to change the explicit terms of a contract. An arbitrator's function is not to rewrite the Parties' contract. His function is limited to finding out what the Parties intended under a particular clause. The intent of the Parties is to be found in the words which they, themselves, employed to express their intent. When the language used is clear and explicit, the arbitrator is constrained to give effect to the thought expressed by the words used."[8]

Hubert Wyckoff: "[Established practice] is a useful means of ascertaining intention in case of ambiguity or indefiniteness; but no matter how well established a practice may be, it is unavailing to modify a clear promise."[9]

Marlin M. Volz: "[I]nherent in every practice is the principle that it is not to be abused and that, if it is, reasonable corrective action may be taken. It cannot be inferred that the other party has accepted or acquiesced in the excesses constituting the abuse so as to make them binding. The employees, no less than management, are under a duty to act reasonably. Both must cooperate and meet the other halfway in following sound industrial practices which will enable the plant to be operated efficiently for the ultimate benefit of the men as well as the Company."[10]

Sidney L. Cahn: "It must be stated as a general proposition that, absent language in a collective bargaining agreement expressly or impliedly to the contrary, once the conditions upon which a past practice has been based are changed or eliminated, the practice may no longer be given effect."[11]

Harry H. Platt: "While, to be sure, parties to a contract may modify it by a later *agreement,* the existence of which is to be deduced from their course of conduct, the conduct relied upon to show such modification must be unequivocal and the terms of modification must be definite, certain, and intentional."[12]

Harry Shulman: "A practice, whether or not fully stated in writing, may be the result of an agreement or mutual understanding. And in some industries there are contractual provisions requiring the continuance of unnamed practices in existence at the execution of the collective agreement. (There are no such provisions in the Ford Agreement or in those of the automobile industry generally.) A practice thus based on mutual agreement may be subject to change only by mutual agreement. Its binding quality is due, however, not to the fact that it is past practice but rather to the agreement in which it is based.

"But there are other practices which are not the result of joint determination at all. They may be mere happenstance, that is, methods that developed without design or deliberation. Or they may be choices by Management in the exercise of managerial discretion as to the convenient methods at the time. In such cases there is no thought of obligation or commitment for the future. Such practices are merely present ways, not prescribed ways, of doing things. The relevant item of significance is not the nature of the particular method but the managerial freedom with respect to it. Being the product of managerial determination in its permitted discretion such practices are, in the absence of contractual provision to the contrary, subject to change in the same discretion. The law and the policy of collective bargaining may well require that the employer inform the Union and that he be ready to discuss the matter with it on request. But there is no requirement of mutual agreement as a condition precedent to a change of practice of this character.

"A contrary holding would place past practice on a par with written agreement and create the anomaly that, while the parties expend great energy and time in negotiating the details of the Agreement, they unknowingly and unintentionally commit themselves to unstated and perhaps more important matters which in the future may be found to have been past practice. The contrary holding would also raise other questions very difficult to answer. For example, what is properly a subject of a practice? Would the long time use of a wheelbarrow become a practice not to be changed by the substitution of four-wheeled buggies drawn by a tractor? Or would the long time use of single drill presses be a practice prohibiting the introduction of multiple drill presses? Such restraints on technological change are alien to the automobile industry. Yet such might be the restraints, if past practice were enshrined without carefully thought out and articulated limitations. Again, when is it a practice? How frequently and over how long a period must something be done before it is to be called a practice with the consequences claimed? And how is the existence of the past practice to be determined in the light of the very conflicting testimony that is common in such cases? The Union's witnesses remember only the occasions on which the work was done in the manner they urge. Supervision remembers the occasions on which the work was done otherwise. Each remembers details the other does not; each is surprised at the other's perversity; and both forget or omit important circumstances. Rarely is alleged past practice clear, detailed and undisputed; commonly, inquiry into past practice of the type that is not the result of joint determination or agreement produces immersion in a bog of contradictions, fragments, doubts, and one-sided views. All this is not to say that past practice may not be important and even decisive in applying provisions of the Agreement. The discussion is addressed to the different claims that, apart from any basis in the Agreement, a method of operation or assignment employed in the past may not be changed except by mutual agreement."[13]

Raymond R. Roberts: "The Company has argued that custom and past practice can never change clear and unambiguous language of the contract. Indeed, the decision between these parties on the Cresswell Grievance, FMCS File No. 78K/11945, November 4, 1978, appears to infer that this is the case.

"Correctly stated, the Parol Evidence Rule excludes any evidence of prior or contemporaneous agreements or understandings which would vary or modify the written terms of the contract. This means that prior or contemporaneous agreements upon which the contract is silent are not foreclosed because they do not vary the written terms of the contract. Such agreements may have been added inducements or consideration to enter into the contract. It also means that agreements that arise subsequent to the adoption of the contract language are admissible to vary the terms of the written contract in order to evidence that the parties subsequently modified the contract or entered into a novation. Accordingly, when the Parol Evidence Rule is invoked it does not exclude all evidence pertaining to the contractual relationship established by the parties other than the written contract, but only evidence of prior or contemporaneous agreements or understandings that would vary or change the written Collective Bargaining Agreement. Willeston Contracts, Section 631; Fox Manufacturing Company, 47 LA 97; Gibson Refrigerator Company, 17 LA 313.

"Some Arbitrators have, as did Mr. Williams as a matter of dictum, held that custom or past practice may never be used to vary the plain and unambiguous language of a Collective Bargaining Agreement. Such statements, in this Arbitrator's view, do not correctly state the Parol Evidence Rule. Because binding custom and past practice is, in reality, an agreement between the parties, binding custom and past practice should be admissible under appropriate circumstances to show that a modification of the contract occurred the same as by any other agreement, whether written or oral. Thus, while the Parol Evidence Rule would exclude evidence of prior or contemporaneous agreements or binding custom and past practice, it would not exclude binding customs or past practices which arose after the contract language was adopted to demonstrate that a modification of the contract was intended and in fact occurred. Fox Manufacturing Company, 47 LA 97; Olin Matheson Chemical Corporation, 40 LA 575; Borg Warner Corporation, 29 LA 625; Houdaille-Hershey Corporation, 22 LA 65; Gibson Refrigerator Company, 17 LA 313; Merrill-Stevens Dry Dock and Repair Co., 10 LA 562. The highest quantum of proof will ordinarily be required in order to show that the parties intended by their conduct to amend or modify clear and unambiguous contractual language, however. Gibson Refrigerator Company, supra.

"In the present case, this view that customs and past practices prescribing benefits for employees could become binding is reinforced by Article XXVII Privileges, which provides:

'No privileges or benefits not herein stated and now being enjoyed by employees shall be discontinued by reason of the execution of this contract.'

"This provision does appear to mandate the continuance of customs and practices which provide benefits to employees over and above those provided by the contract."[14]

William Eaton: "It is axiomatic that where language is clear and unambiguous, an arbitrator must give that language effect. . . . '[N]evertheless, an arbitrator is confined to interpretation and application of the Collective Bargaining Agreement; he does not sit to dispense his own brand of industrial justice. He may, of course, look for guidance from many sources, yet his award is legitimate only so long as it draws its essence from the Collective Bargaining Agreement. When an arbitrator's words words manifest an infidelity to this obligation, courts have no choice but to refuse enforcement of the award. (Steelworkers v. Enterprise Wheel and Car Corporation, 363 U.S. 593, 80 Sup. Ct. 1358, 34 LA 569, (1960).' . . . '[A]n Arbitrator cannot resort to interpretation or construction if there is no ambiguity in fact' in the language being construed. 'To do otherwise' Arbitrator Shipman stated, 'would in effect, be to change or alter the Agreement through indirection,' which the arbitrator was not empowered to do. Lionel Corp., 9 LA 716, 717–718 (1948).' Other arbitrators have agreed that past practices are of *no* probative value when the language is unambiguous and definite. See: Union Carbide Corp., 70–1 ARB Sec. 8098 (1969), Weather Seal Division of Georgia Pacific Corp., 70–1 ARB Sec. 8247 (1969), Exxon Chemical Company, 68 LA 362 (1977), Kennecott Copper Corp., 70–2 ARB Sec. 8849 (1970), Duriron Company, Inc., 51 LA 185 (1968)."[15]

William W. Petrie: "'Whatever particular words may ordinarily mean, a totally different sense must be ascribed to them if the actions of the parties indicate plainly that such was what the parties understood.' The case held that 'words cannot be read in a vacuum,' and that arbitrators 'frequently recognized that they have no recourse but to look at more than the literal language to ferret out true contract meaning.' Waukegan News-Sun, 74 LA 1063, 1065 (1980). See also: Black Oak Restaurant, Inc., 63 LA 479 (1974), Kaiser Aluminum & Chemical, 43 LA 898 (1964), Tecumseh Products Co., 65 LA 762 (1975), I-T-E-Imperial Corp., 67 LA 354 (1976), La Favorite Rubber Mfg. Co., 70 LA 1048 (1978), Tenn-Tex Alloy and Chemical Corp., 43 LA 152 (1964). . . . The general rule which would appear to emerge from these and similar citations is that it is always the intent of the parties which the arbitrator is obliged to ascertain. Normally, the intent is best and most clearly expressed in the written collective bargaining agreement. However, it is clear that in other cases, normally the exceptions, it may be equally clearly expressed by the actions. . . . Such (a) practice(s), post-dating the language at issue, is as clearly a contracting act as the writing of the language . . . the Arbitrator is obliged to follow the most recent expression of the contracting intent of the parties. . . ."[16]

Wayne C. Hatcher: "In the face of diametrically opposed positions, the Arbitrator has resorted to other authorities to ascertain what other arbitrators expressed as to when a past practice is in evidence, if at all, and what elements normally are to be found before a past practice is to be given full credence, considering that there is an absence of language in the agreement specifically dealing with the situation to be resolved. . . . [(Citing Volz in 74−2 ARB Para. 8618 (1974)]: "Several requirements for a custom or practice to supply an omission are well established. First in order for it to rise to the dignity of equality to a contractual provision, the same mutuality and the same meeting of minds on the essential terms of the practice are required as in the negotiation of a written provision. The assumptions and expectations of one party do not establish a binding practice. Both sides must have reasonable cause to believe that what has been done in the past will be continued in the future in the precise situation. . . . [C]onsistency and repetitiveness is another characteristic of a binding practice. . . . For a practice to ripen into an established past practice . . . it must be followed with such consistency and over such a period of time that the employees may rely and reasonably expect such practice to continue. . . . A third fundamental notion is that consistency and the repetitiveness are not controlling where they apply to the exercise of a power specifically granted by the parties to the Company. In such instance the Company in the discretionary exercise of that power may do so consistently...."[17]

Thomas J. McDermott: "Whether that past practice is enforceable will depend on the contract. If there is contract language relating to the issue, but it is ambiguous or vague, the established past practice gives the meaning to that language, under certain circumstances, where a contract is silent, the establishment of the existence of the practice becomes in effect an unwritten agreement, which makes the practice a part of the labor agreement between the parties."[18]

David A. Singer, Jr.: "The paramount issue is clear. On the one hand, the right of management to conduct its enterprise must be protected. Of equal significance is the legitimate influence of past practice over present and future practice.

"At what point does past practice give way to management's right to conduct its enterprise? Under most circumstances arbitrators have held past practice to be enforceable, and have viewed such practice as a part of the 'whole' agreement fashioned by the parties. Arbitrator Jones (Alpena General Hospital, 50 LA 48, 51) articulated a definitive statement on the issue of past practice. 'It is generally accepted that certain, but not all, clear and long standing practices can establish conditions of employment as binding as any written provision of the agreement.' See also: Jacobs, 9 LA 197, 198; Volz, 39 LA 1265, 1269; McCoy, 16 LA 73, 74; Merrill, 24 LA 191–195.

"Where custom is enforced there is always implied mutual agreement between two parties. Therefore, custom or past practice exerts a possible source of limitation upon management's rights. However, management's rights must be preserved, and such preservation is as crucial to the Union as the Company...."[19]

Roger I. Abrams: "A past practice is a mutual unwritten understanding between a union and management, evidenced normally by repeated consistent conduct responses to similar situations. Customary benefits and working conditions of personal value to the workers can ripen into binding obligations when they have become engrained in the common practice of the workplace. By comparison, core managerial prerogatives involving methods of operation or the direction of the working forces, when not expressly controlled by contractual provisions, are generally not subject to treatment as binding practices. In the absence of evidence that the parties to a collective relationship had consciously explored and reached an understanding on such an issue, there simply is no basis for finding a binding obligation. 'Such practices are merely present ways, not a prescribed way, of doing things.' Ford Motor Co., 19 LA 237, 242 (Shulman, 1952)."[20]

Barry J. Baroni: "It is a well recognized arbitral principle that the contractual relationship between the parties normally consists of more than the written word. Existing practices, dealing with major conditions of employment, are to be regarded as included within a collective bargaining agreement negotiated after the practice has become established and not repudiated or limited by it. Negotiators are assumed to work within the framework of existent practice and must be taken to be conscious of it. (See: Metal Specialty Co., 39 LA 1265, 1269 [1962]; Phillips Petroleum Co., 24 LA 191 [1955]). For a matter to be given 'binding practice' effect as an implied term of the agreement, it must be well established and strong proof of its existence will ordinarily be required. In the absence of written documentation, for past practice to be binding on both parties, it must be (1) unequivocal; (2) clearly enunciated and acted upon; (3) readily ascertainable over a reasonable period of time as a fixed and established practice accepted by both parties. The mutual acceptance may be tacit and inferred from circumstances. (See: Caraway in 72 LA 253; Updegraff in 20 LA 243; 'the party alleging the existence of a binding practice has the burden of proving it,' Duff in 75 LA 1216. Ray in 48 LA 919, and Heinsz in 74 LA 50; Sass in 78 LA 766; Cohen in 78 LA 241; Gootnick in 72 LA 733; Caraway in 72 LA 253; 'Awareness of a practice is to be presumed from its long-established and widespread nature"; Valtin in 33 LA 374; and Levy in 76 LA 620.) The line between practices which are binding and those which are not may well be drawn on the basis of whether the matter involves methods of operation or direction of the working forces, or whether it involves a 'benefit' of peculiar personal value to the employees (though also involving the employer's purse). Arbitrators are often hesitant to permit unwritten past practice or methods of doing things to restrict the exercise of legitimate functions of management (e.g. assignment of work). However, arbitrators have often ruled custom to be binding where it involved a benefit of peculiar personal value to employees. Some of these benefits include paid work breaks, bonuses, various monetary benefits, and benefits that are part of the wage structure. (See: *How Arbitration Works* [Fourth Edition], Elkouri and Elkouri, Student Edition, pp. 444-445).

"The Union's central argument is one of custom and past practice. The specific past practice is one involving 'peculiar personal value' to employees—the continued reversion of health and welfare contributions back to the employee for overtime hours worked. This opinion will consist of a detailed analysis of the specific Contractual provisions; peculiar facts relating to this establishment and existence of the practice alleged by the Union; and the effect of such a practice, once established, upon the contractual relationship between the parties and their commitments to one another....

"*Effect of the Established Practice:* If the new Appendix 'A' was intended by the Company to deprive unit employees of the reversion of the welfare contributions, the clause would have so stated a specific exclusion. In the absence of such a clear and unambiguous deletion of the reversion practice, the Company bears the burden (not that the Union has borne its burden of proving the existence of the established practice) of proving that the omission in the new Contract of the language found in Article VIII, Section 6, was indicative of the Company's intent to change the established practice of reverting the health and welfare contributions for overtime. The language omission, standing alone, did not accomplish that proof. Hence, the Contract language found in Appendix 'B' which limits health and welfare contributions to 40 hours of work is in direct conflict with the established practice which places no such limitation on health and welfare contributions for hours worked over 40 hours per week on overtime. The conflict and confusion must be resolved in favor of unit employees and against the Company, since (1) the Company was remiss in not proceeding properly to challenge the established practice in negotiations, and, (2) the Company is responsible for preparing the drafts of new contracts, and could have resolved the present ambiguity in the contractual relationship existing between the parties by more exactness of expression in its preparation of the drafts of the 1984 Agreement. In effect, the entire contractual relationship consists of the language of the 1984 Contract and the established practice in effect which pre-dates the new Agreement and which was not specifically repudiated by it...."[21]

Appendix B: Labor Arbitration Reports

Following is a list of arbitration cases dealing with the role of custom and past practice in labor relations, published by the Bureau of National Affairs, Inc., Washington, D.C., in their publication *Labor Arbitration Reports*.

In General

51LA40
51LA705
52LA771
52LA1155
53LA405
53LA1024
53LA1078
53LA1317
54LA686
54LA947
54LA1093
58LA557
58LA887
59LA106
59LA980
60LA473
60LA482
60LA838
62LA258
62LA544
63LA789
63LA805
63LA810
63LA845
63LA867
63LA869
64LA651
64LA705
64LA707
64LA889
65LA165
65LA887
65LA993

65LA1177
66LA1207
67LA103
67LA759
67LA920
67LA1175
69LA87
69LA1057
71LA595
71LA921
71LA929
71LA1136
72LA258
72LA1047
73LA188
74LA1063
74LA1191
75LA137
75LA1112
76LA62
77LA492
77LA1287
78LA865
79LA123
81LA179
82LA889
82LA1020
83LA767
83LA883
83LA1281
84LA53
84LA185
85LA1034

Working Conditions
62LA179
62LA708
62LA819
62LA1123
62LA1127
63LA483
65LA88
65LA982
65LA1219
66LA190
66LA227
66LA413
66LA485
66LA1026
67LA147
67LA368
67LA989
67LA1109
68LA94
68LA547
68LA745
68LA1223
69LA678
70LA278
70LA360
70LA938
70LA1003
71LA61
71LA852
72LA588
72LA594
72LA863
72LA876
72LA1079
72LA1296
72LA1302
73LA107
73LA330
73LA837
73LA949
73LA1007
74LA770
74LA964
74LA1055
74LA1169
75LA523
75LA1211
76LA333
77LA8
77LA14

77LA44
77LA545
77LA705
77LA1027
77LA1088
77LA1145
79LA272
79LA618
80LA568
81LA249
81LA749
82LA117
82LA538
82LA735
83LA529
83LA602
83LA1047
85LA476
85LA874

Bonuses
56LA1256
59LA344
62LA209
62LA637
62LA879
64LA571
65LA1121
67LA493
73LA924
77LA1220
81LA529
82LA755
85LA738

Discharge or Discipline
51LA287
51LA549
51LA759
51LA813
51LA1266
52LA33
52LA176
52LA528
52LA639
52LA707
52LA1273
53LA69
53LA584
53LA1325
54LA52

Appendix B

54LA311	51LA813
54LA376	51LA1266
54LA613	52LA33
54LA642	52LA176
54LA701	52LA528
54LA1155	52LA639
55LA184	52LA707
55LA1130	52LA1273
56LA957	53LA69
56LA1296	53LA584
57LA1085	53LA1325
57LA1121	54LA52
57LA1174	54LA311
58LA1219	54LA376
58LA1343	54LA613
59LA828	54LA642
59LA837	54LA701
60LA118	54LA1155
60LA821	55LA184
60LA1147	55LA1130
66LA705	56LA957
67LA660	56LA1296
70LA809	57LA1085
71LA129	57LA1121
72LA1	57LA1174
72LA804	58LA1219
72LA1285	58LA1343
74LA252	59LA828
75LA154	59LA837
76LA62	60LA118
76LA114	60LA821
76LA140	60LA1147
76LA719	61LA229
76LA827	61LA360
76LA1120	61LA689
77LA845	61LA891
77LA1259	61LA920
78LA665	62LA45
80LA902	62LA96
80LA1243	62LA226
81LA361	62LA627
82LA1107	62LA706
83LA253	62LA794
83LA1138	63LA400
85LA962	63LA645
	64LA19

**Hours; Premium Pay;
Break Periods; Overtime**

51LA287	64LA71
51LA549	64LA179
51LA759	64LA549
	64LA984
	65LA864

66LA183
66LA769
66LA1065
67LA747
68LA51
68LA1264
69LA14
69LA115
70LA590
70LA1303
71LA504
71LA544
71LA676
71LA702
71LA1055
71LA1128
72LA253
72LA364
72LA668
73LA172
73LA391
73LA677
73LA827
73LA1200
74LA699
74LA827
74LA884
74LA1142
74LA1214
75LA47
75LA241
75LA275
75LA492
75LA633
75LA653
75LA1183
75LA1241
76LA848
76LA1261
77LA23
77LA393
77LA464
77LA474
77LA626
77LA657
77LA853
77LA1017
78LA241
78LA729
78LA819
78LA885

78LA1241
79LA313
79LA636
79LA926
80LA730
80LA1146
81LA338
81LA461
81LA667
81LA1060
82LA283
82LA620
82LA805
83LA59
83LA124
83LA440
83LA445
83LA561
83LA807
83LA889
83LA895
83LA1029
83LA1049
83LA1162
84LA190
84LA252
84LA537
84LA553
84LA736
84LA998
84LA1125
84LA1231
85LA425
85LA615
85LA1013
85LA1107

Job Classifications & Rates

54LA1180
56LA332
57LA633
62LA684
63LA254
65LA114
66LA941
66LA1081
68LA311
68LA908
69LA687
71LA692
73LA846

74LA144
74LA1072
83LA811
84LA235

Layoffs

51LA705
52LA368
64LA589
65LA283
65LA771
65LA1191
65LA1280
73LA1083
76LA516
76LA739
77LA96
79LA505
79LA1075
79LA1205
80LA118
80LA1188
80LA1279
81LA73
81LA953
81LA1184
82LA193
83LA346
84LA225
84LA627
84LA629
84LA1198
85LA41
85LA398

Pensions & Insurance

53LA1332
54LA335
54LA472
55LA277
56LA1061
60LA69
60LA316
61LA145
62LA1056
63LA281
63LA479
63LA965
64LA756
64LA1132
64LA1172

65LA7
65LA228
65LA645
65LA1260
66LA655
67LA421
68LA1208
69LA740
72LA1013
72LA1300
73LA540
74LA20
75LA534
76LA241
76LA456
76LA620
76LA986
77LA905
78LA205
81LA616
81LA1139
83LA249
84LA1198
85LA137
85LA1100

Seniority; Promotion;
Transfers; Job Vacancies

52LA79
52LA568
52LA633
52LA993
52LA1051
53LA901
54LA555
54LA593
54LA824
55LA23
55LA79
55LA270
57LA91
57LA527
58LA1041
59LA523
60LA61
62LA84
62LA535
62LA549
62LA800
62LA887
63LA692

63LA959
63LA1026
64LA316
64LA589
65LA449
65LA538
65LA790
65LA825
65LA1191
66LA342
66LA844
67LA354
67LA582
67LA702
68LA114
68LA708
70LA346
70LA729
70LA1048
71LA647
71LA789
72LA340
72LA874
72LA1175
72LA1279
73LA669
73LA729
73LA892
73LA990
73LA1218
74LA514
74LA1077
75LA306
76LA208
76LA773
76LA825
76LA1017
77LA49
77LA402
77LA689
77LA831
78LA548
78LA1114
78LA1137
79LA48
79LA493
79LA658
79LA868
80LA499
80LA623
80LA625

80LA1118
81LA51
81LA649
81LA797
81LA946
81LA1122
81LA1126
82LA528
82LA866
84LA18
84LA194
84LA325
84LA346
85LA329
85LA489
85LA877
85LA894
85LA958
85LA962

Sick Leave & Sick Benefits

51LA645
51LA799
52LA608
52LA728
53LA63
53LA293
53LA799
53LA1019
54LA1269
58LA199
58LA613
62LA35
62LA736
62LA909
63LA834
63LA982
64LA239
70LA470
71LA1208
72LA229
74LA1142
75LA623
76LA241
76LA875
76LA1261
78LA940
79LA1220
81LA639
81LA1139
83LA21

83LA66
83LA394
84LA21

Subcontracting

75LA665
77LA1096
84LA1037
85LA594

Union Business

52LA644
55LA773
57LA970
61LA925
62LA1219
63LA378
66LA49
66LA197
70LA887
73LA630
73LA872
74LA501
74LA1055
75LA66
75LA1011
76LA1142
76LA1273
80LA528
80LA950
81LA467
81LA852
84LA593
85LA913
85LA1140

Vacations; Holidays; Leaves of Absence

51LA268
51LA289
51LA400
52LA857
52LA1134
53LA941
54LA869
54LA1146
55LA6
55LA628
56LA43
58LA1280
60LA51

60LA128
60LA865
60LA1137
60LA1320
61LA187
61LA635
61LA958
62LA472
62LA1056
63LA507
63LA1096
63LA1282
64LA103
64LA1155
64LA1300
65LA795
65LA1105
66LA192
66LA399
67LA666
67LA997
68LA925
68LA1000
69LA115
69LA431
69LA665
69LA674
69LA944
70LA669
70LA693
70LA1046
71LA43
71LA214
71LA937
71LA1034
71LA1039
71LA1068
72LA408
72LA534
72LA1104
73LA414
73LA547
73LA607
73LA1144
73LA1146
74LA50
75LA814
75LA1067
75LA1076
75LA1216
76LA60

76LA554
76LA611
76LA673
76LA1007
77LA342
77LA706
78LA1021
79LA449
79LA576
79LA1294
80LA41
81LA191
81LA254
81LA764
81LA943
81LA994
81LA1220
81LA1268
82LA177
82LA193
82LA405
82LA448
82LA469
82LA819
82LA825
82LA1329
83LA8
83LA305
83LA973
84LA84
84LA137
84LA265
84LA438
84LA891
84LA894
85LA162
85LA382
85LA398
85LA425
85LA640
85LA700
85LA1109

**Wages; Benefits;
Incentive Plans; Report Pay**

52LA904
52LA921
53LA92
53LA845
54LA716
54LA721

54LA1159
56LA237
57LA470
58LA127
58LA719
60LA95
60LA609
60LA875
60LA1050
60LA1221
61LA473
61LA1135
61LA1286
62LA854
62LA955
62LA1018
62LA1128
62LA1258
63LA159
63LA261
63LA569
63LA1280
64LA17
64LA547
64LA760
64LA864
64LA997
65LA731
65LA773
65LA836
65LA947
65LA1121
65LA1215
66LA988
68LA20
68LA362
68LA547
68LA845
68LA855
68LA1022
68LA1110
68LA1129
69LA198
69LA562
69LA756
70LA124
70LA530
70LA690
70LA1256
71LA606
71LA1031

72LA190
72LA288
72LA333
72LA380
72LA470
72LA479
72LA1232
73LA172
73LA623
73LA924
74LA5
74LA333
74LA865
74LA1030
74LA1169
75LA18
75LA29
75LA135
75LA519
75LA1208
76LA267
76LA446
76LA911
76LA1236
77LA237
77LA990
77LA1045
77LA1058
77LA1151
77LA1153
79LA334
79LA1205
79LA1333
80LA229
80LA787
80LA931
81LA80
81LA249
81LA726
81LA749
81LA1181
82LA476
82LA500
82LA898
83LA59
83LA124
83LA361
83LA541
83LA657
84LA163
84LA337

84LA764
84LA1055
85LA377
85LA500
85LA905
85LA1064
85LA1109

Work Assignments

51LA41
52LA23
52LA440
52LA473
52LA648
52LA749
52LA880
52LA1098
53LA234
53LA836
53LA965
54LA184
54LA647
54LA1080
55LA19
55LA41
55LA464
57LA889
58LA1182
60LA38
60LA770
61LA797
61LA1253
61LA1305
62LA695
62LA805
66LA1201
67LA113
67LA1154
69LA1133
70LA563
71LA48
71LA59
71LA238
72LA795
73LA126
73LA529
73LA1123
73LA1264
74LA15
74LA132
74LA543

75LA106
75LA462
75LA540
75LA988
76LA424
76LA535
76LA601
76LA867
76LA903
77LA415
77LA876
77LA937
78LA401
78LA660
78LA819
79LA362
79LA415
79LA430
79LA578
79LA792
79LA1097
80LA771
80LA855
80LA1211
81LA378
81LA421
81LA483
81LA584
82LA170
82LA244
82LA689
82LA846
82LA910
82LA942
82LA1026
82LA1030
82LA1100
82LA1244
83LA74
83LA346
83LA415
83LA621
83LA685

83LA1205
83LA1270
84LA203
84LA422
85LA81
85LA521
85LA585
85LA669
85LA958

Work Schedules

51LA490
51LA1102
52LA351
52LA987
53LA1342
54LA588
61LA984
65LA323
66LA543
66LA1201
67LA113
67LA1154
69LA1133
70LA563
72LA410
72LA639
73LA418
75LA16
77LA49
79LA1087
80LA1108
81LA483
81LA911
82LA1073
84LA361
84LA369
84LA978
85LA256
85LA780
85LA790
85LA988

Chapter Notes

1. Exclusive Agreement Clauses

1. See 43LA1262.
2. Labor agreement between International Association of Machinists, Local 1813, and Brunswick Corp., Technical Products Division.
3. See 37LA297.
4. *Ibid.*
5. See 29LA372.
6. *Ibid.*
7. See 45LA470.
8. See 19LA421.
9. See 32LA516.
10. See 21LA398.
11. See 17LA382.
12. See e.g., *Sacramento Navigation Co. vs. Salz,* 27U.S.326.
13. See 10LA272.
14. Labor agreement between Rubber Workers and Samsonite Corp., Murfreesboro, Tenn.
15. See 26LA627.
16. See 30LA100.
17. See 16LA115.
18. *Ibid.*
19. See 3LA254.
20. *Ibid.*
21. See 24LRRM1518; 35LRRM2709; 36LRRM2716.
22. See 22LRRM2564.
23. See 28LRRM1443.
24. See 31LRRM1220.
25. See 41LRRM2089.

2. Clear Language Versus Conflicting Practices

1. See 15LA713.
2. See 27LA605.
3. See 22LA628.
4. See 23LA289.
5. See 21LA325.
6. See 21LA650.
7. See 13LA556.
8. See 21LA699.
9. See 21LA230.
10. See 7LA86, Arbitrator George Cheney.

11. See 11LA380, Arbitrator Ralph T. Seward; similarly, 12LA217.
12. See 17LA313, Arbitrator Harry H. Platt.
13. See 22LA191.
14. See 22LA628.
15. See 22LA628.
16. See 27LA229.
17. See 22LA883.
18. See 43LA322.
19. See 18AAA11.
20. See 31LA240.
21. See 44LA698.
22. See 19AAA17.
23. See 24AAA3.
24. See 4AAA16.
25. See 19AAA16.
26. See 17LA524.

3. Benefit Versus Gratuity

1. See Archibald Cox and John T. Dunlop, "The Duty to Bargain Collectively during the Term of an Existing Agreement," *Harvard Law Review,* vol. 63 (1950), pp.1116–1117.
2. See 6LRRM786.
3. See 66LRRM2634.
4. See 63LRRM1151.
5. See 65LRRM1126.
6. See 59LRRM1270.
7. See 72LRRM1309, decision rendered October 15, 1969.
8. See 20LA276.
9. See 44LA1034.
10. See 10LA664.
11. See 21LA515.
12. See 44LA118.
13. See 10LA79.
14. See 32LA388.
15. See 24LA500.
16. See 25LA853.
17. See 32LA395. For additional cases of arbitral rulings supporting the company's position regarding past practice and its impact on the continuance of a benefit, see 10LA541 and 668; 9LA472; 45LA897; 32LA999 and 40LA239.
18. See 34LA592.
19. See 45LA277.
20. See 37LA381.
21. See 37LA831.
22. See 44LA467.
23. See 44LA66.
24. See 17LA395.
25. See 39LA964.
26. See 32LA228.
27. See 30LA35.
28. See 39LA72.

29. See 17LA505. For additional cases where the rulings favor the union, see 36LA1228, 41LA1238, 42LA5333, 35LA929, 18LA276, 32LA228, 21LA194, 3LA194, 37LA375, 10LA577, 44LA1025, 33LA375, and 39LA1188.
30. See 45LA353.
31. See 45LA92.
32. See 32LA139.
33. See 32LA395.
34. See 34LA586.
35. See 42LA765.
36. See 10LA804. For additional cases, see 38LA216; 10LA46; 32LA664.
37. See 53LA405.
38. See 35LA503.
39. See 34LA732.
40. See 42LA415.
41. See 45LA34.
42. See Cox and Dunlop, "Duty to Bargain," pp. 1097, 1116, 1118.

4. Past Practice Versus Management Rights

1. Labor Agreement between United Rubber Workers Local 779 and Samsonite Corp., Murfreesboro, Tenn.
2. See 43LA608.
3. See 13LA949.
4. See 30LA1265.
5. See 36LA160.
6. See 27LA6.
7. See 27LA123.
8. See 18LA320.
9. See 18LA620.
10. See 28LA538.
11. See 15LA840.
12. See 22LA680.
13. See 38LA5.
14. See 39LA588.
15. See 43LA970.
16. See 41LA169.
17. See 41LA464.
18. See 41LA765.
19. See 42LA466; see also 42LA781.
20. See 45LA840.
21. See 45LA1062.
22. See 39LA180; see also 39LA552.
23. See 40LA1193; see also 34LA200.
24. For cases involving this aspect, see 26LA438 and 27LA57.
25. See 22LA404 for cases involving this factor.
26. See 27LA233.
27. See 27LA174; also, 19LA815.
28. See 26LA723 and 22LA124.
29. For cases involving this factor, see 30LA678 and 29LA609.
30. For cases involving this factor, see 27LA671 and 21LA330.
31. See 31LA701.
32. See 23LA210.

33. See 40LA240.
34. See 39LA676.
35. See 47LA1045.
36. See 6LA565.
37. See 44LA359.
38. See 44LA1134.
39. See 45LA889.
40. See 42LA224.
41. See 39LA65.
42. See 22LA289.
43. See 18LA827.
44. See 19LA237.
45. See 45LA104.
46. See 44LA1230.
47. See 3LA560.
48. See 30LA444.
49. See 24LA73.
50. See 35LA637.
51. See 28LA704.
52. See 39LA321.
53. See 36LA691.
54. See 31LA200.
55. See 46LA289.
56. See 38LA273.
57. See 36LA92.
58. See 17LA105.
59. See 15LA688.
60. See 10LA50.
61. See 3LA482.
62. See 42LA1287.
63. See 34LA99.
64. See 28LA274.
65. See 21LA699.
66. See 39LA93.
67. See 36LA1464.
68. See 36LA129.
69. See 44LA725.
70. See 41LA1042.
71. See 36LA1044.
72. See 36LA166.
73. See 10LA43.
74. See 38LA49.
75. See 35LA228.
76. See 42LA525.
77. See 36LA1257.
78. See 12LA217.
79. See 35LA945.
80. See 35LA109.

5. Standards Determining a Fixed and Established Past Practice

1. See Institute of Industrial Relations, University of California, 1960, *(Law & National Labor Policy)*, vol. 12, p. 143.
2. See 28LA439.
3. See 28LA14.
4. See 17LA81.
5. See 29LA372.
6. See 3LA137; see also 3LA760.
7. See 29LA256.
8. See 1LA313.
9. See 23LA277.
10. See 29LA555.
11. See 27LA762.
12. See 27LA793.
13. See 9LA197.
14. See 21LA524.
15. See 22LA835.
16. See 10LA617.
17. See 29LA45.
18. See 23LA27.
19. See 15LA87.
20. See 10LA786.
21. See 23LA562.

Appendix A: Representative Arbitral Commentary

1. See 39LA1265.
2. See 9LA197.
3. See 50LA48.
4. See 16LA73.
5. See 49LA423.
6. See 24LA191.
7. Mittenthal, "Past Practice and the Administration of the Collective Bargaining Agreements"; 14 Annual NAA (BNA 1961).
8. See 16LA229.
9. See 17LA829.
10. See 39LA1265.
11. See 34LA99.
12. See 17LA313.
13. See 19LA237.
14. See 78LA729.
15. See 79LA658.
16. See 77LA780.
17. See 69LA665.
18. See 74LA1072.
19. See 80LA950.
20. See 80LA1273.
21. See 88LA735.

Bibliography

Aaron, B., Davis, W., and Bailer, R. "The Uses of the Past," in *Arbitration Today* (BNA Books, 1955), pp. 1–24.

American Federation of Labor–Congress of Industrial Organizations. *AFL-CIO Manual for Shop Stewards.* Washington, D.C.: AFL-CIO, 1982.

Anderson, Howard J. *Primer of Labor Relations,* 21st ed. rev. Washington, D.C.: BNA, 1980.

Baer, Walter. *Labor Relations Guidebook.* Dubuque, Iowa: Kendall/Hunt, 1978.

Beall, Edwin F., Wickersham, Edward D., and Kienast, Philip. *The Practice of Collective Bargaining,* 4th ed. Homewood, Ill.: Richard D. Irwin, 1972.

Bergman, Paul. *Trial Advocacy in a Nutshell.* St. Paul, Minn.: West, 1979.

Boyce, Timothy J. *Fair Representation, the NLRB, and the Courts.* Philadelphia: Wharton School, U. of Penn., 1978.

Brodewe, Paul. *Expendable Americans.* New York: Viking, 1974.

Bureau of National Affairs. "Management Rights and the Arbitration Process," in *Proceedings of the Ninth Annual Meeting of the National Academy of Arbitrators.* Washington, D.C.: BNA, 1956.

――――――. *Grievance Guide,* 5th ed. Washington, D.C.: BNA, 1978.

Chamberlain, Neil W. *Collective Bargaining.* New York: McGraw-Hill, 1951.

――――――. "Management's Reserved Rights," in *Management Rights and the Arbitration Process* (Washington, D.C.: BNA, 1956), pp. 118, 145–147.

――――――, and Kuhn. *Collective Bargaining,* 2nd. ed.

Code of Professional Responsibility for Arbitrators of Labor-Management Disputes. National Academy of Arbitrators, American Arbitration Association, and Federal Mediation and Conciliation Service, Washington, D.C., 1974.

Coulson, Robert. *Labor Arbitration—What You Need to Know.* New York: American Arbitration Association, 1978.

Cox, Archibald, and Dunlop, John. "The Duty to Bargain Collectively During the Term of an Existing Agreement." 63 *Harvard Law Review* (1950), pp. 1097, 1116–1117.

Crawford, Donald. "Challenge to Arbitration," in *Proceedings of the Thirteenth Annual Meeting of the National Academy of Arbitrators* (Washington, D.C.: BNA, 1960).

Davis, William. "Arbitration of Work Rules Disputes." 16 *Arbitration Journal* (1961), p. 51.

Dennis, D., and Somers, Gerald G., eds. *Arbitration—1977. Proceedings of the 38th Meeting of the National Academy of Arbitrators.* Washington, D.C.: BNA, 1978.

Elkowri, Frank, and Elkowri, Edna. *How Arbitration Works,* 3rd ed. Washington, D.C.: BNA, 1973.

Fairweather, Owen. *Practice and Procedure in Labor Arbitration,* 2nd ed. Washington, D.C.: 1983.

Fossum, John A. *Labor Relations: Development, Structure, Process.* Dallas: Business Publications, 1979.

Goldberg, Arthur J. "Management's Reserved Rights: A Labor Review," in *Proceedings of the Ninth Annual Meeting of the National Academy of Arbitrators* (Washington, D.C.: BNA, 1956).

Grossman, Mark M. "The Question of Arbitrability," in *Industrial and Labor Relations* (Ithaca: Cornell University, New York State School of Industrial and Labor Relations, 1984).

Harrison, Allan J. *Preparing and Presenting Your Arbitration Case: A Manual for Union and Management Representatives.* Washington, D.C.: BNA, 1979.

Hegland, Kenney F. *Trial and Practice Skills in a Nutshell.* St. Paul, Minn.: West, 1978.

Hill, Marvin, Jr., and Sinicropi, Anthony. *Evidence in Arbitration.* Washington, D.C.: BNA, 1980.

Hobgood, William P., and Gifford, Courtney D. *Directory of U.S. Labor Arbitrators.* Washington, D.C.: BNA, 1985.

Inwiukelried, Edward J. *Evidentiary Foundation.* Charlottesville, VA.: Michie, 1980.

Jeans, James W. *Trial Advocacy.* St. Paul, Minn.: West, 1975.

Jox, Marshall J. *Lawyers' Concise Guide to Trial Procedure.* Englewood Cliffs, N.J.:Prentice-Hall, 1965.

Justin, Jules J. *How to Manage with a Union.* Industrial Relations Workshop Seminars, 1969.

Kagel, Sam. "Anatomy of a Labor Arbitration." Washington, D.C.: BNA, 1961.

Kestler, Jeffrey L. *Questioning Techniques and Tactics.* Colorado Springs, Colo.: Shepards/McGraw-Hill, 1982.

Lawson–United Feldspar and Mineral Co. 16 LRRM 1558 (NLRB–1971).

Levin, Edward, and Grody, Donald. *Witnesses in Arbitration.* Washington, D.C.: BNA, 1987.

Lloyd-Bostock, Sally, and Clifford, Brian R. *Evaluating Witness Evidence.* New York: John Wiley, 1983.

Loftus, Elizabeth F. *Eyewitness Testimony.* Cambridge: Harvard University Press, 1979.

Lyd, Staughton. *Labor Law for the Rank and Filer.* San Pedro, Calif.: Singlejack, 1982.

McElhaney, James W. *Trial Notebook.* Chicago: American Bar Association, 1981.

McLaughlin, John. "Custom and Past Practice in Labor Arbitration." 18 *Arbitration Journal* 205 (1963).

Marceau, Leroy, ed. "Dealing with a Union." 169 AMA 142–156.

_____. *Drafting a Union Contract.* Boston: Little, Brown, 1965.

Marshall, James. *Law and Psychology in Conflict.* New York: Bobbs-Merrill, 1980.

Maver, Thomas A. *Fundamentals of Trial Techniques.* Boston: Little, Brown, 1980.

Meltzer, George. "Ruminations About Ideology, Law, and Labor Arbitration," in *Proceedings of the Twentieth Annual Meeting of the National Academy of Arbitrators* (Washington, D.C.: BNA, 1967).

Mettenthal, Richard. "Past Practice and the Administration of Collective Bargaining Agreements." *Arbitration and Public Policy* 30 (1961), pp. 32–33.

Morrill, Alan E. *Trial Diplomacy,* 2nd ed. Chicago: Court Practice Institute, 1983.

Murphy Diesel Co., 179NLRB27, 1970.

National Academy of Arbitrators. *Proceedings of the Annual Conference on Labor Arbitration, 1948 through Present.* (Washington, D.C.: BNA).

National Lawyers Guild. *Guide to Labor Law for Employees and Union Members.* New York: Clark Boardman, 1981.

O'Barr, William M. *Linguistic Evidence.* New York: Academic Press, 1982.

Repas, Bob. *Contract Administration.* Washington, D.C.: BNA, 1984.

Ryder, Meyer S. "Problems and Issues Involving the Private Adjudication of Bargaining Unit Work Coverage Disputes." 14 *Labor Law Journal* 839 (1963).

Sayles, Leonard R., and Strauss, George. *The Local Union,* rev. ed. New York: Harcourt, Brace and World, 1967.

Schaffner, Margaret Anna. *Labor Contracts from Individual to Collective Bargaining.* Madison: University of Wisconsin Press, 1907.

Scheinman, Martin F. *Evidence and Proof in Arbitration.* Ithaca, NY.: ILR Press, 1977.

Shulman, H. "Reason, Contract and Law in Labor Relations." 1968 *Harvard Law Review,* 999.

Sonsteng, John O., Haydock, Roger S., and Boyd, James J. *The Trial Book.* St. Paul, Minn.: West, 1984.

Stern, James L., and Dennis, Barbara D., eds. "Truth, Lie Detectors, and Other Problems in Labor Arbitration," in *Proceedings of the Thirty-First Annual Meeting of the National Academy of Arbitrators* (Washington, D.C.: BNA, 1979).

Stone, Morris. *Employee Discipline Arbitration.* New York: American Arbitration Association, 1977.

————. *Labor Grievances and Decisions.* New York: American Arbitration Association, 1970.

Trotta, Maurice S. *Arbitration of Labor-Management Disputes.* New York: AMACOM, a Division of American Management Association, 1974.

————. *Handling Grievances: A Guide for Management and Labor.* Washington, D.C.: BNA, 1976.

United Steelworkers vs. Warrior & Gulf Navigation Co. S. Ct. 1347; 1351–1352 (1960).

Updegraff, Clarence M. *Arbitration and Labor Relations,* 3rd ed. Washington, D.C.: BNA, 1970.

Wellman, Francis L. *The Art of Cross-Examination,* 4th ed. New York: Collier, 1962.

Werne, Beryamew. *Administration of the Labor Contract,* 3 vols. Mundelein, Ill.: Callaghan, 1963.

Zack, Arnold M. "Arbitration in Practice," in *Industrial and Labor Relations* (Ithaca: Cornell University, New York State School of Industrial and Labor Relations, 1984).

Index